You Can Make More Money Now!

More Than
150 Proven Ways
To Generate Income

Including Basic, Creative
and Extreme Methods to Make Money

By
Dr. Larry A. Maxwell

Author of
More than 500 Proven Ways to Reduce Expenses
More than 200 Extreme Ways to Reduce Expenses

More Than 150 Proven Ways to Generate Income

More Than 150 Proven Ways to Generate Income

Dedicated to
All those struggling to make ends meet.

More Than 150 Proven Ways to Generate Income

Special thanks to Michael Skelly.

Disclaimer - Though the author, his family, friends, or people he knows successfully applied ideas in this book, if you choose to apply any of these you do it at your own risk with no warranty of effectiveness in the context of your specific situation. The author and the publisher do not accept any responsibilities for your actions. The author does not receive any compensation from any company or product mentioned in this book.

Published by 1775 Productions
1130 Perry Rd., Afton, New York
599 Route 311, Patterson, New York

GoodInformation.US

Cover Design by Matthew Reid Maxwell

ISBN: 978-1-949277-06-7

COPYRIGHT © 2019 - LARRY A MAXWELL

More Than 150 Proven Ways to Generate Income

Table of Contents

Section	**Page**
Introduction	7
Additional Employment	9
Find Money or Items of Value	18
Sell Merchandise	36
Make Money with Things You Make	62
Make Money with Food	78
Services You Can Sell	107
Write & Publish	145
Entertainment Related	159
Miscellaneous Ways	172
Extreme Ways to Generate Income	174
Important Considerations	181
About the Author	193
Index	195

More Than 150 Proven Ways to Generate Income

Introduction

Do you need, or want, to generate additional income right now? Are you are facing economic difficulties and desperately need more money? Maybe you just want to find a way to get some extra money to spend. Or, perhaps you desire to generate additional income to improve your standard of living. If any of those statements apply, this book was designed to be of help to you.

No matter how old you are, whether you are eight years old or eighty, and no matter how much education you have, this book contains methods you may be able to use to generate the additional income you need or desire.

The first thing you should consider is, can you reduce your expenses? If you reduce your expenses that makes more income available to you. I wrote two books which provide practical help for that, they are: *More Than 500 Proven Ways to Reduce Expenses;* and *More Than 200 Extreme Ways to Reduce Expenses.*

Generating income can be a challenge. I know many people who work hard but are not generating the income they need or want. A wise person once told me, there is a difference between working *hard* and working *smart*. I discovered sometimes I was working *hard* but not working *smart*. Hopefully you will find some *smart* ways to generate income in this book.

Many of the methods in this book can work for anyone willing to put them to work. Some can provide additional income almost instantly. Some take longer to produce results. Some of these methods can help you generate a little extra income while others can be used to generate a significant amount of money.

I know people who use methods presented in this book to generate more than enough income to support their families.

Some of the income generating methods found in this book are quite simple. Some are more complex and explained in greater detail. Some of them are fun and provide opportunities for friends and family members to work together.

One of the most helpful resources for generating additional income is having time you can use to generate that income. Almost everyone has some free time. The more time you have available the more opportunities you will have to generate more income.

The reason many of the methods in this book can generate income for you is the fact many people are willing to pay someone else to do things for them.

Most of the income generating methods in this book do not require any special skills. Some require simple skills, but most people can learn those skills. I avoided listing methods which require advanced skills.

Some methods in this book will be considered extreme by some people, but they work and may work for you.

As you read this book you may notice I try to insert some humor to lighten things up. Hopefully you will distinguish between when I am being serious and when I am using some sarcasm.

I have two warnings for you. **First**, read the Important Considerations Section at the end of this book. There may be some legal requirements you need to consider before you undertake some methods in this book. **Second,** if you follow one of these methods and start to generate a significant amount of money, do not leave a paid job until you generate enough income over a significant period of time to consistently support yourself.

As time passes, and the world changes, it is possible some of the methods presented in this book will no longer work. Why not apply one of the methods in this book now, while they work, and start to generate some significant income?

Find Additional Employment

This first category for generating additional income is usually the most traditional way and the first item many people consider, so it is addressed first.

Finding additional or different employment can often provide a consistent source of income for an extended period of time, or it can be utilized temporarily.

Some of the methods in this category can be accomplished almost immediately. Some take a longer amount of time. Some can generate income on a part-time basis, some work better on a full-time basis.

If seeking additional employment is not what you are looking for, there are number of other ways in this book which you can use to generate additional income.

1. Work Additional Hours.

For many people, one of the first ways to generate additional income is to work additional hours.

If You Work for Someone Else.

Can you work additional hours? Perhaps you can come in an hour or two earlier and/or stay an hour or two later, one or more days a week.

Some employers are open to this idea if you are a good worker. If you know your job it can cost them less to have you work extra hours instead of hiring an additional employee.

Many states require employees to be paid at a higher rate for overtime. That is a drawback for some employers, yet it is a benefit for you.

If You Work for Yourself

If you work for yourself consider adding one or two more hours to your work day. You may need to add additional clients.

2.   Work an Additional Day.

Many people work five days a week. That is a relatively new idea. Years ago, most people worked six or seven days a week. I do not recommend working seven days.

If it is possible, you may want to add an additional day to your work schedule to generate the additional income you need or want. Just make sure you do not make the mistake of spending too much time working. You must learn to balance your priorities and make sure you allow time for other important things

During the Industrial Revolution people often worked seven days a week. Thanks to the efforts of Robert Raikes and others it was discovered people who worked six days instead of seven were more productive.

Though you may be able to work seven days, it is important you do not work at least one day a week. The Bible teaches you should not work more than six days in a week. That is good advice. It wisely instructed people to set aside one day to worship, rest and spend time with family.

3.   Work a Different Shift.

You may want to consider working a different shift. Many jobs pay different rates depending on which shift you choose. Often working the second or third (graveyard) shift pays more than the traditional first shift.

One person I know, who works for the New York City Police Department, choose the graveyard shift because it pays significantly more than the other shifts.

4.   Transfer to a Different Location.

The cost of living varies greatly from place to place. In New York State there are places where the cost of living is three to four times higher than in other parts of the state.

If your company has jobs in a different geographic area, with a lower cost of living than where you live, you may want to consider asking for a transfer. Some companies will pay employees to move to other areas.

Even if you are paid the same salary, or slightly less in that other location, if the cost of living is significantly less than where you live now, you will have additional income because your expenses will be lower.

5.   Drive for a Transportation Service.

It is very possible you could generate some immediate income being a driver for other people. You may be able to do this on an on-call basis with a transportation company. If you do this with a service like *Uber* or *Lift* you can start now and drive whenever you are available.

You may not need a special driver's license to drive for a service unless you are driving a limousine, bus, or van.

If you drive for a service, you need a decent reliable good-looking car, a good driving record, and a helpful personality.

Customers often book their rides with a service company. The service dispatches drivers, like you. You do the transport and are paid electronically, often the same day or week.

With some transports, such as to an airport, you may be able to get an additional client on the return trip.

6.   Go to a Temporary Agency.

There are temporary (temp) employment agencies which may be able to get you some work today. Those agencies often have you fill out an extensive application with your experience and interests. That helps them match you with job opportunities. Sometimes they can get you a job you never dreamed of.

One time I was between jobs and needed some immediate income. A temp agency found me a job that same day working as an accountant at a prestigious ski shop. Another time a temp agency found a job for me at a very nice hotel. I did not know I had experience which was helpful for either of those jobs.

7.   Get a Second Job.

Sometimes it may be necessary for you to get a second job. There are many part-time job opportunities. Depending on your skill set and abilities, you can work for someone else or work for yourself

If you want to work for yourself there are many ways you can do that which are addressed in this book.

If you follow the route of securing a second job make sure the job you select does not conflict with your current job or with your other responsibilities. It would be terrible to gain more income and lose your family.

8.   Be a Process Server.

Many civil court cases require people be served in person with legal papers. People who do that are called *Process Servers*.

This is a job you can do part-time or full-time. They are often paid between $30 to $250 per paper served. Many earn between $25,000 to $70,000 per year.

Process Servers are provided with known addresses for people and then must locate them and serve them with the court papers by a specific date.

In most cases they do not need to secure the signature of the person being served. They only have to present them with the papers in person and then fill out a form describing the person, along with the place and time the papers were served.

This is not always an easy job. Some people do not want to be found and try to avoid being served papers. You must be prepared to protect yourself from angry people.

9.   Repossess Vehicles & Boats.

I was in a repair shop one day when two men came in and talked about repossessing a car that day. They said they went to a courthouse, found the car they were looking for and drove off with it. They told me they were paid $250 for each vehicle they retrieved. They said they retrieved multiple vehicles every week.

When people fall behind on their car or boat payments the companies holding the loan eventually get the legal authority to repossess the vehicle. Companies hire people to go and repossess the vehicles for them.

Sometimes the companies contact the people who are behind on their payments and the person willingly gives up the vehicle or boat. A person is then sent to pick it up.

Sometimes the person is unwilling to surrender the vehicle or boat, then someone must go take it. The person sent to pick it us is provided work and home addresses as well as keys to the vehicle and papers authorizing them to repossess the vehicle.

This usually pays between $150 to $450 per vehicle. Many possessors collect four to five vehicles per week.

10.   Drive for Car Resellers.

I had a pastor friend who went to auto auctions and bought cars to resell. He paid people to come with him to drive the cars home which he bought at the auction.

If you know of some auto resellers in your area you may want to offer your services as a driver.

11.   Be a Pallbearer or Attendant.

Funeral Homes hire people to serve at funerals. Some are full-time positions paying between $18,000 to $42,000 per year. Many hire part-time people on an hourly or per funeral basis.

Some work as attendants to help at the funeral, or as pallbearers to carry the coffin when there are not family or friends who want to do that task.

You need a nice black suit, white shirt and tie and need to look good in a suit. If you can look sad and sympathetic, that is even better.

If you work for a Jewish funeral home they will provide

a *kippah* (skull cap).

To secure such a position, wear a nice conservative, dark outfit and contact local funeral homes in person to see if they are hiring.

12.   Be a Paid Mourner.

If you like funerals and like to comfort people perhaps you could generate income being a *Moirologist*. A *Moirologist* is a professional paid mourner. This is a historical profession with roots in the Mediterranean. *Moirologists* are hired to attend funerals and mourn for the departed. Some read touching eulogies. These people make a person seem more popular.

More importantly, those who provide this service provide comfort to the family as they see people who appear to care about the passing of their loved one.

Rent-a-Mourner in England pays mourners $68 to attend a funeral for two hours. According to a *Radio Netherlands* report, some professional mourners earn two hundred dollars a day attending funerals.

If you want to be a professional mourner, you must learn to tastefully show sorrow and concern. Understand how important your role is and how much it means to those attending a funeral to see people who appear to be deeply touched by the passing of their loved one.

If you must speak as a mourner, make sure your employer preps you with some things to say. Be brief. Some will advise you that if anyone asks you how you knew the departed, it is best to and say, *I'm sorry,* and walk away as though you are overcome with grief. Never lie. If you talk too much or make up things, you are on a slippery slope and may end up doing more harm than good.

13.   Be a Roadkill Collector.

This is a necessary but very stinky and unromantic job. Every day thousands of animals are killed on roads and highways and need to be removed. This is a job very few people want so there may be opportunities for you to do this in your area.

If you do this you must be aware on oncoming traffic. It is best to wear a *Class 3 Safety Vest*. You should also wear gloves and protective clothing.

This works best with a pickup truck. Some dead animals are heavy and require ropes and some kind of lift system. After picking up the roadkill you usually need to take it to an approved disposal facility.

A *CNN* report stated a roadkill collector in Pennsylvania was paid $40 for removal of each deer killed. He averaged removing 1,800 dead deer a year earning $72,000.

Some roadkill collectors arrive on the scene shortly after an animal is killed and are allowed to keep whatever meat they can salvage. I have a section on roadkill in my book, *More than 150 Extreme Ways to Reduce Expenses*.

There are two other way to make money from roadkill addressed in this book, one is **Find and Sell Antlers**. The other is addressed under **Sell Hides**.

14. Get a Different Job.

Sometimes one of the hardest truths to accept is the fact you may need to change jobs.

According to a 2017 Survey by the *Society of Human Resource Management*, two out of five employees expressed a desire to change jobs within the next year.

If you do not find your current job fulfilling, and especially if it does not meet your financial needs, you probably need to change jobs.

You should do a personal financial inventory before you consider changing jobs. If you discover your current job does not meet your financial needs and personal goals, then take steps to find if there is a better job for you.

Consider taking a career interest survey or speak with a career counselor.

The Princeton Review offers a career test. I took their test. It was very simple, and its results were very accurate. On the other hand, I took a more detailed test from *WhatCareerIsRightForMe.com* and the results did not match my interests at all.

I recommend you get advice about a possible career change from reliable people you know and trust. I do not recommend you discuss this with your employer or fellow employees, unless you are discussing different job opportunities within the same company.

I also recommend you consider the advice given by the Apostle James. He said, if you need wisdom, ask God and God will give you that wisdom. James is saying God exists and cares about you and wants to help you. If God does exist, and I believe He does, imagine having a wise supernatural being, who knows you better than you know yourself, willing to help you. James says there is a caveat for this to work, when you ask God for wisdom, you must approach Him not asking for options but with a heart willing to do what He shows you. I seek that wisdom all the time and often find it.

15. Apply for a Government Job.

Many government jobs pay well and provide good benefits. Many governments, especially in The United States of America, claim to be equal opportunity employers. After numerous lawsuits the government lowered qualifications for many jobs to allow almost anyone breathing to qualify. You probably qualify for quite a few government jobs.

No matter what politicians say or promise, they all seem to allow government to grow bigger and bigger, so the number of government jobs keeps growing every year. Hence the greater chance you may be able to get a job with the government.

A number of years ago Air Traffic Controllers went on strike. They were government employees and were forbidden to strike. The government fired all of them and quickly sought to hire replacements. I applied for one of those jobs. I had no background in that field but was offered a position.

In many cases, government jobs do not pay as well as those in the public sector, but some pay more. Government jobs often have better benefits and have high job security, no matter how well you do the job. A sad truth is many promotions in government jobs are not based on performance but on longevity or political favoritism.

16.   Run for Elected Office.

Running for some elected offices will provide you with additional income while giving you a chance to help your community. Some elected positions are full time and pay very well. Some are part-time and still pay quite well.

This is usually not a quick way to generate income because you have to wait for an election and then run for office and win the election. However, you can earn money while running for office, even if you are not elected.

Some people run for elected office and never get elected yet pay themselves a salary from their campaign. That is allowed according to the *Federal Election Commission*.

If you run for office and are elected you may receive a salary and some benefits.

In the county where I live, they pay the part-time County Legislators a salary which is equivalent to what the average person earns who lives and works full-time in the county.

Our state pays its part-time legislators a salary higher than the average person earns in our state. After only five years of service they qualify for a pension.

If you are elected to the U.S. Congress, the pay in 2018 was $172,443. You will also receive health care and other benefits. If you serve as a congressman for five years, or as a senator for six years, you earn a pension.

Find Money or Items of Value

Have you ever wanted to be a treasure hunter? When I was a young boy and lived on Long Island, my friends and I heard about pirates who buried treasure on that island. We dreamed about finding one of those treasures. Wouldn't that be a great way to generate some income?

Though you may not find a buried pirate's treasure, if you are willing to put in some effort, it is very likely you can generate some income immediately by finding some items of value and then selling them.

Some of these methods presented here may seem insignificant but people generate a significant amount of income finding things of value and reselling them.

With most of these methods it is a very good idea to write down where and when you found the particular item. That can add significantly to its resale value.

17. Find Coins.

Every day people drop coins in parking lots, on sidewalks, or in other places. Many people do not bother to bend down and pick those up. Sometimes the coins roll under an object, such as a vending machine, making them more difficult to retrieve. All that dropped coinage becomes unclaimed money waiting to be claimed by anyone who is willing to look for it and pick it up.

In 2014, the United States Mint estimated at least $3.08 billion of coinage was dropped.

When I was in High School I worked at Jones Beach for three years. I discovered people dropped coins every day, especially near the vending machines. The coins often rolled out of sight and remained unretrieved. Every time I walked by the vending machines I looked underneath them. Sometimes the coins were easy to reach. Other times I used a small broom to retrieve them. I recovered between $5-10 of coins every week. That was back when machines took mainly nickels and dimes. Now most machines require quarters or dollar coins, so there is a greater potential to find coins of more value.

Coin operated telephones were another good source for coins. People often did not realize some coins were returned in the coin return on the phone. I found that true in America and in other countries as I travelled. Many times, I found more than $1 worth of coins in pay phones. One time I found $5 worth of coins in one phone. I found enough coins in a pay phone in France to pay the train fare from the airport to see the *Eifel Tower*. It is too bad there are not as many pay phones around now as there were years ago but there are still some.

During his morning walk, a man in Florida would walk past a self-serve car wash and check the machines for change. He found more than $5 each time. At the end of ten years he found a total of more than $21,000.

A family in New Paltz, New York, decided to pick up any change they saw on the street and put what they found in a jar. At the end of a year they collected $1,003.

18.   Look at Your Change.

Some coins you receive as change are worth more than their face value. There are a few reasons for that. People who get into financial difficulties spend coins they saved. Others inherit a jar of old coins and have no idea how valuable they are and spend them. People on drugs steal coin collections and use the coins for their face value.

When I was growing up some teens broke into our home and stole my father's proof coin collection. They broke open the sets and spent the coins at a local *7 Eleven* for face value. Some people received those valuable coins as change for their face value.

If you pay with cash as you shop it is possible you may end up with some valuable coins as change.

I use a simple method to sort change during the day. Coins I receive, which might have extra value, I place in my left pocket; the rest go in my right pocket.

Some Coins to Look For:

Silver Coins.

All U.S. coins made 1964 or before, except nickels and pennies, contain silver.

The 1964 Kennedy half-dollars were made of 90% silver. The 1965-1970 Kennedy half-dollars were made of 40% silver.

The price of silver fluctuates. As I write this, the value of the following coins based on their silver content alone (not collector value) are:

Dime = $1.13 each.	10 = $11.30
Quarter = $2.82	10 = $28.20
1964 Half Dollar = $5.65	10 = $56.50
1965-1970 Half Dollar = $2.31	10 = $23.10

Indian Head/Buffalo Nickels.

Indian Head Nickels, also called Buffalo Nickels, were minted between 1913– 1938. They have a buffalo on one side and the head of an American Indian on the other side.

If you cannot read the date, value = 15 cents.
With a readable date = $7 to $70,000

Wheat Pennies (1909-1956)

Wheat Pennies are a copper penny featuring a bust of President Lincoln on one side and sheaves of wheat on the other.

Wheat Pennies = $0.04 to $1,000.00 each.

In 1943, during World War II, they were minted in steel.

Steel Penny value = $0.04 to $10

Some 1943 pennies were minted in copper by mistake. There are very few. One sold at auction for more than $1 million.

Some 1944 pennies were minted in steel by mistake. The last one sold at auction for $158,623.

Pennies from 1957 to 1982.

Pennies minted between 1957 and 1981 contain 95% copper. Part way through 1982 the U.S. Mint started to issue pennies composed of 97.5% zinc, with a thin copper coating.

Some copper ones were still minted in 1982. The 1982 copper pennies weigh 3.11 grams and make a high-pitched *ring* sound when dropped. The 1982 zinc pennies weigh 2.5 grams and make a *klunk* sound when dropped.

Copper pennies range in price from $0.02 to $10,000.

Current copper melt value, as this is written, is about two cents each. That may not sound like much, but it adds up.

    100 pennies face value = $1.
    The copper value for 100 is about $2.

Imagine if someone handed you $100 and it was actually worth $200. Save 1982 and older pennies and that is what happens.

Collector Coins or Unique Coins

If a coin looks unique set it aside and look up its value later. You will never know what treasure you may have received until you look it up.

19. Find, Collect & Redeem Bottles & Cans.

This method is a standard way some people use to generate significant extra income. It can be used by both children and adults. This method works because many people do not want to be bothered redeeming cans and bottles.

In 2016, $102 million of deposits were unclaimed in New York State. That does not count the millions of dollars people earned returning bottles and cans.

In many states a deposit is charged whenever anyone

purchases a carbonated beverage, or water. in a bottle or a can. The current standard deposit charge is $0.05, no matter what size the container.

If a person returns one of those bottles or cans, they receive the deposit money. You do not have to be the one who made the purchase to redeem it.

Some retailers only accept returns of bottles or cans from the manufacturers they sell. There are some places called *Redemption Centers* which issue refunds for any deposit bottle or can returned. Those *Redemption Centers* are not to be confused with churches with that name.

This was one of my favorite ways to generate income when I was younger. I collected bottles from neighbors and brought them back to the local grocery store where they gave me $0.02 per small bottle and $0.05 for large ones. I then used the money and bought a six-pack of full-size *Hershey* chocolate bars for $0.25.

The method has significantly exploded with the amount of people using disposable water bottles.

Redeeming bottles not only helps you but also helps our environment.

Collect These from Neighbors

Many people do not want to bother returning bottles or cans which have a deposit on them. Ask them if you can have them.

Find Them Near the Road

We did a roadside liter clean up as a community service project. We started to carry a bag just for deposit bottle and cans. It was not unusual to collect $3-5 worth of cans and bottles in one hour.

If you go out and just look for deposit bottles, like some people do, and do not pick up the additional trash as we did, you may be able to collect even more in the same amount of time.

Sort Through Waste Cans & Dumpsters

That is too extreme for some people. The best place is

in municipal areas. Some municipalities allow this.

I have seen people doing this in *New York City* with a police officer standing nearby and smiling. Some municipalities like Denver have ordinances against this.

Make sure you find trashcans you can easily access. Never do this on private property.

Be very careful if you decide to climb into dumpsters to do this. You never know what, or who, you will find in there.

As you collect bottles you will find some containers with liquid in them. No matter how thirsty you are, NEVER take a drink from one of them.

20. Pan for Gold.

One day, while living in New Hampshire, as I was driving home I saw a man standing in the river with a shovel. It was common to see people fishing there but I was sure this man was not fishing with a shovel. I stopped and asked him what he was doing. He told me he was panning for gold. I was surprised because I thought that was something people only did out west or in Alaska. I asked if he ever found gold. He produced a vial which contained about $300 of gold which he found that day.

After that, I bought a gold pan, built a sluice box, and began panning for gold. I discovered there was not only gold in that river but some nice minerals too.

If you want to pan for gold, do some research. You will find there are specific places listed on various websites where you can find gold.

21. Find & Sell Rocks & Minerals.

Those who hunt for rocks and minerals are often called *Rock Hounds*. Collecting rocks and minerals is a nice rewarding hobby. It is something you can do alone or with family and friends. It makes a hike more interesting when you look for minerals. You may also be able to make some money selling the rocks and minerals you find.

After I learned how to pan for gold and discovered there were also minerals in the same river, I went to a local mineral shop to ask some questions about my find. While in that shop a man walked in with a box of minerals, which he gathered in the nearby mountains. The shop owner paid him $300 for his find. That aroused my interest.

After that, I was told a druggist at a small pharmacy was an avid rock collector. I went to visit him.

When I asked him if he was a rock collector he looked at me sternly and asked, *Do you have rocks in your head?*

I looked back at him with a smile on my face and said, *Yes!* He then smiled and said, *That is the right answer.*

He then showed me some of his collection. When he saw I was genuinely interested, he told me where I could find valuable *twin staurolite crystals* less than five miles from his shop.

I also had the privilege to meet another man in that area who found one of the largest *smoky quartz* crystals ever discovered, less than three miles from where I was living. That quartz crystal was worth thousands of dollars.

Learn which rocks and minerals may be found near where you live and then go hunt for some. Some people do research and plan rock hunting vacations.

Rocks and minerals vary greatly in price. Some sell for a few dollars and some sell for millions. You may sell them to dealers, at shows, at Flea Markets or online. Always label them with where they were found.

22. Find & Sell Meteorites.

More than 18,000 meteorites, larger than 10 grams in size, fall to earth every year. They are usually pieces which break off from larger asteroids. When they are moving in space they are called *meteors*. When they enter our atmosphere, they are called *meteorites*.

Meteorites can be found almost anywhere on the planet and are waiting to be discovered. They can sell for $5,000 to $25,000 each. Some sell for many times more than that.

You need to do some research to learn what they look like and to discover places where you will have a greater chance of finding them.

Do you know what they call people who study meteors? Though it would seem they should be called *meteorologists*, that name refers to someone who studies the weather. A person who studies meteors is called a *meteoricist*.

Many *meteoricists* belong to The *Meteoritical Society*. That society maintains an online database of places where meteorites have been found.

Some meteorites give off low levels of radioactivity when they first land. Scientists say such levels are not dangerous. If you find a meteorite which recently landed scientists may be interested in studying your find.

If you find green meteorites do not call Superman.

If you go hunting for meteorites there are two helpful tools to bring with you:

Metal Detector

Most meteorites contain metal so bring along a metal detector. It works best if you set it to look for gold.

Meteorite Finding Stick

Most meteorites are magnetic so a meteorite finding stick has a magnet on one end. You can make one of these yourself.

23. Find & Sell Fossils.

Fossils can be found in many places all over the world. Many people collect fossils and will pay for good samples.

Prices of fossils vary greatly. They depend on the size and rarity of a fossil.

One piece of *Canadian Amorite* was found which sold

for $158,000.

In 2015, one *T-Rex* fossil was valued at $12.5 million.

I love finding fossils and have found fossils in many different places. Some of my best success has been in New York and Pennsylvania along riverbeds with lots of shale. Yet I also found them on top of the Rocky Mountains.

A person who studies fossils is called a *paleontologist*. If you want to be successful at finding fossils to sell you need to be an *amateur paleontologist*. You need to be familiar with what fossils look like and where to find them.

Some museums host Fossil Identification Days, similar to the television show, *Antiques Roadshow*. They let you bring your fossils to find out what they are. Proper identification of what you have found will help you sell them better.

As with other items you find to sell, it is very important to label fossils with the location where they were found. If you add some background information about the fossil that can greatly affect its value.

Hunting for fossils is also a great family activity. I love to hunt for fossils along the creek near my wife's childhood farm. It is fun to see the joy come across people's faces when they find a fossil. That is a priceless experience.

24. Find & Sell Seashells.

Growing up in a town next to the Atlantic Ocean I saw many seashells along the beach. I took them for granted until I visited some gift and craft shops in other areas and discovered people pay for seashells.

If you are ever at a gift shop near a beach you may see a woman going into the shop with a bag of sea shell. That is probably because she sells seashells by the sea shore.

Seashells were used as jewelry and currency by some tribal people.

Many varieties of seashells are used as jewelry. *Abalone* shells are often used by jewelers to make cameos.

There are many different types of seashells. They come in all different sizes. Some are quite fragile and break easy. Undamaged ones usually sell for the most, so be careful as you collect and transport them.

Some seashells break in the sea and become smooth in the ocean current. Some of those can be collectable. That also happens with glass. Smoothed beach glass is also sellable. Also look for shark teeth and dried starfish.

If you find a closed oyster shell you may open it and find a pearl inside. According to the *Pearl Source Blog*, natural pearls range in value from $300 to $1500. Some people take diving trips to try to find pearls.

You may want to multi-task and do a combination of metal detecting and collecting seashells.

You can sell seashells or make sea shell arrangements to generate more money.

25. Find & Sell Driftwood.

Many people like driftwood. Driftwood is wood which has drifted in the water for a period of time. It may be tree branches or parts of old ships. The waves and currents usually smooth the ends of the wood and make beautiful looking driftwood.

The price driftwood sells for depends on its size and the way it looks. Some sell for a few dollars, some sell for hundreds of dollars.

Collect all sizes. Some people make furniture out of driftwood or use them for decoration and receive thousands of dollars for their creations.

26. Find & Sell Artifacts & Relics.

Many people like historical artifacts and relics. I have met some relics who became good friends.

You can look for historical artifacts or relics (the non-people ones) as an *amateur archaeologist*. You can do this near where you live, or you can travel to different places looking for them.

Many people compare old maps and new maps to find old abandoned places to investigate.

Some items may be found above ground yet may are covered and need to be carefully unearthed.

As with many other items, it will increase the value of an item if you label it with the location where it was found. If you add some brief historical background that also may add some additional value.

Arrowheads

Most arrowheads were made with stone until the Europeans came. Then some were made with metal.

Some people I know are very good at finding these. If you find some, try to add information about the tribe which lived in the area.

Overstreet publishes an *Indian Arrowhead Guide* showing the value of various arrowheads.

One of the most expensive arrowheads was a Clovis Point which sold at auction in 2009 for $276,000.

Musket Balls & Bullets

Musket balls and bullets are popular finds. They are made of metal and can be found with a metal detector. Ones found near battlefields are usually considered more valuable.

The specific location where these are found, and some history of the area add more value to them.

Cannon Balls

Cannon balls are not as plenteous as musket balls and bullets but are easier to find. I have a diver friend who found many cannon balls.

If you can provide historical background you can sell some for a few hundred dollars.

If you find a cannon ball with a sealed plug be very careful, it may have powder inside which can still explode, even if it is more than 200 years old.

Buckles & Buttons

Old buttons and buckles are made of various materials, but most are made of metal and can be found with a metal detector.

There are many books which can help you identify the buttons you find.

Military buttons, especially ones with regimental numbers or letters, are usually worth more than civilian buttons.

Buttons with maker's marks can sell for $200 each.

Some rare buttons sell for hundreds of dollars.

Old Nails

Older buildings were made with hand forged nails. The body of older nails are usually square or rectangular.

Some only sell for $1-2 but you can usually find quite a few at a time.

27. Find & Sell Old Bottles.

There is a market for old glass bottles or ceramic crocks. They vary greatly in value. As with many other items, the older ones are usually worth more.

You can buy these at flea markets or tag sales, but you will usually make more money if you do some exploring and find them laying around.

When I was in college I visited a friend during spring break. He had a friend who hired me to help him paint skylights on top of apartment building in Albany, New York. One day, he asked me if I would like to go digging for old bottles with him. It sounded interesting, so I said yes.

We went to an island in the Hudson River which was an old abandoned garbage dump. He looked for mounds. Then he had us gently dig in them. We recovered enough old bottles to fill a box. He said they were worth about $300. We also found two ceramic crocks. He said one would sell for $100 and the other for $300.

One day, while visiting my in-laws in Pennsylvania, I was walking along an old dirt road on a hill above a stream. I looked over the edge of the road and saw a bottle covered by some leaves. I climbed down the hillside and uncovered the bottle. It was more than 50 years old. I was surprised to find another bottle underneath it which was even older. Then I found another bottle under that. I found four different bottles one on top of the other. The lowest one was more than 100 years old. It appears someone walking or riding along that road tossed a bottle over the side and it landed next to the tree without breaking. Leaves built up and created a cushion to receive the second bottle and then the next. The process continued over the years until I uncovered them.

I have often found old bottles at garage sales and flea markets. Those can be good places to sell them. Learn to identify valuable bottles and to detect reproductions.

28.   Find & Sell Strands of Barbwire.

I was surprised when I learned some people collect old barbwire. There is an *Antique Barbed Wire Society*.

In November 1853, W. H. Meriwether of New Braunfels, Texas, filed a patent for his barbed wire. In 1867 Lucien B. Smith filed a patent for a different style.

Farmers used barbwire to keep livestock in and to keep unwanted game and uninvited guests out. It was hated by cowboys and cause many feuds between them and farmers. Some called it *Devil's Rope*.

You can find and sell strands or make nice displays of barbed wire and sell them for even more.

29.   Find & Sell Old Barnboard & Beams.

Barnboard is weathered siding from old buildings and barns. There is quite a market for that.

Builders and designers like large quantities of long wide barnboards which they can use for a project. Smaller quantities and individual pieces can be sold to artists, decorators, and crafters.

Barnboard values vary from $5 to $12 per foot.

There is also a demand for old large beams, especially the old hand-hewn ones. These are often used as decorative pieces and can be sold individually. The wider, longer and more pieces you have the greater your return.

Old wood beams vary from $8 to $20 per foot.

Look for old buildings in your area, preferably 50 to 100 years old or older. Many times, people will pay you to take them down.

This can be labor intensive, and some boards are quite heavy. You will probably need some help to undertake this profitable income generating method.

30. Find & Sell Old Windows.

One day I saw some old windows by the side of the road with the word *Free* on them. I thought perhaps I could use them to replace some broken windows in my old barn, so I picked them up. I was disappointed when I discovered they were the wrong size.

When we had a tag sale I put the windows out with a sign on them which read, *Make an Offer*. A woman offered me $10. There were 10 windows and they were taking up space, so I thought $10 for something which cost me nothing was a good offer. She handed me $100 and thanked me for such a good deal. She paid me $10 per window. I asked her what she intended to do with the windows. She said she was an artist and painted on them and resold them. Though I was happy with the $100, she was happier because they were worth much more to her.

Old windows with leaded or blown glass windows can sell for hundreds of dollars. The leaded glass has a wavy appearance. The blown glass often has bubbles in it and is the most valuable.

Many people remodel their homes and replace windows. The would rather give them away for free than pay to dispose of them.

You may want to contact local window contractors and offer to take away old windows. You could sell them to artists or may want to try your hand at being an artist.

31.   Find & Sell Railroad Spikes.

Many old railroad lines crisscross the country. Old spikes, known as *rail holders* or *rail fasteners* hold railroad ties in place. Some of the oldest ones are called *Dog Spikes* and many are historical artifacts.

There are about 10,000 spikes used per mile of track, so they are quite abundant. Over the years, spikes come loose and need to be replaced. It was a common practice for railroad crews to throw the old spikes along the side of the tracks. In many places these pieces of history lay there waiting for someone to pick them up.

I have collected railroad spikes from many different railroad lines across the country.

It is best to gather these on abandoned railroad lines. There are some old rail lines which are active. Gathering spikes along those can be dangerous and may be forbidden in some areas.

Most railroads run on two parallel rails. If you see a third rail in the middle of a line STAY AWAY! That third rail carries a dangerous amount of electricity to power some trains and can kill you.

There are people who collect and will pay for railroad spikes and other railroad items. You can also collect them and sell them as scrap metal. In some places they are worth $1 to $2 each as scrap.

Many spikes have imprints on their heads. Those help identify where they were made. People like to collect spikes with different imprints. Older spikes are smaller and more valuable.

These spikes can be sold to crafters. Perhaps you could use these to make some crafts to resell.

32. Find & Sell Telephone Insulators.

Starting in the 1850's telephone wires crossed the country running from pole to pole. They were wrapped around heavy glass insulators to protect the integrity of the signal. The old glass insulators are heavy sold glass pieces which come in a variety of colors. They are labeled with manufacturer information. They were later replaced by ceramic and then plastic insulators.

Many old phone lines are abandoned, and old telephone poles dot the landscape with old insulators still attached. Many have fallen down and are very accessible.

Some people collect those insulators. They usually want a variety of colors and ones from different parts of the country. They sell for $2 to over $400 each.

Some use them as candleholders or paper weights. Some people use them as crafts. One creative project is to use them as a hanging lamp or a row of lights. Those often sell for hundreds of dollars.

33. Find & Sell Antlers.

Deer, Moose and Elk shed their antlers in cold climates every winter and regrow new ones in the spring. In warmer climates they shed them in the spring.

Some people gather antlers and resell them. Others make furniture and art work out of them. That can generate some significant income.

You have to look for antlers shortly after they are shed because rodents often eat them. Deer often shed both antlers within three days and often within the same area. If you find one antler, expand your search in a radius out from that point. Look on the ground where they may be hidden by leaves. They may also be in bushes or lodged in low lying branches.

Antlers are easier to find on rainy days because they have a shine to them when wet.

When Deer, Moose and Elk die from wounds or natural

causes they may leave behind a carcass with the head and both antlers intact. You may be able to make such finds. Those are more valuable than individual antlers..

You may also collect some antlers from roadkill.

Deer and Elk antlers sell for $6 to $12 per pound. Some large Elk antlers can weigh 40 pounds. Moose antlers retail for about $25 a pound. They can weigh more than 50 pounds. A matching set are more valuable.

You can generate more income if you make a display or furniture with antlers.

34. Locate Lost Items.

Some people lose items and do not have the time to try to find them and are willing to pay a reward for those who do. Look at classified ads in newspapers and online sites such as *Craigslist*.

As I wrote this I found someone listed a $10,000 reward to anyone who could find their two dogs and return them. Some classified only state, *Cash Reward*.

Some countries have laws which provide a finder's fee of 5-10% of the value of the item.

If you find lost items, such as wallets or phones, for which no reward is offered, do the right thing, and return them, even if you only get a thank you.

35. Find People.

Many people would like to connect with people they have lost contact with or want to find undiscovered relatives. Many people are unaware how to do that and will pay others who can help them locate someone.

The internet makes the task of finding people a lot easier. You can learn how to do that.

I do people searches and have been very successful primarily using *Google Search*, *Google Image Search*, *Facebook*, school alumni sites, obituaries, *AnyWho.com* and online newspapers.

36. Be a Bounty Hunter.

Being a Bounty Hunter is an extreme version of finding people, yet usually pays much more and usually requires some training and requires a license in some states.

Bounty Hunters look for people wanted by the police. Some are like the Old West where there is a reward posted for a criminal. More commonly Bounty Hunters make their money locating *Bail Jumpers*.

Bail Jumpers locate people who were arrested, appeared in court, and were released on bail. They signed a bail bond waiving their constitutional rights and agreeing if they do not appear in court they may be arrested by a *Bail Bond Agent*.

If they do not show up in court, when required, they have *jumped bail*. They forfeit the bail money and become wanted by the police.

People who locate bail jumpers are Bail Bond Agents. They are also called *Bail Enforcement Officers* or are more commonly known as *Bounty Hunters*.

Bounty Hunters often earn 10-20% of the bail bond. Some bounty hunters average $50,000 to $80,000 per year. Sometimes there is a more significant reward.

Bounty Hunters can be very effective locating and arresting people. They apprehend many more bail jumpers every year than police officers. That may be due to the fact they do not face the restrictions place on police officers. Bounty Hunters do not need warrants. They only need a copy of the Bail Piece or a certified copy of the bond. They can enter private dwelling unannounced if they know the bail jumper is present.

It is important to know the local laws regarding bounty hunting in the state you plan to do this. Anyone who wants to become a Bounty Hunter should get some basic training, though that may not be required in some areas. Arizona requires only a 20-hour training course, whereas California requires a 40-hour course. Those courses are very helpful and will let you know the law and your rights and how much force you can legally use to arrest a person.

Make sure you check the local laws where you want to be a Bounty Hunter. Some states require Bounty Hunters be licensed. Some require them to be registered. Some do not allow bounty hunting. Some require police or military background. Some states have few regulations.

Bounty hunting comes with significant risks. Many people who are wanted by the police do not want to be found. That makes bounty hunting more difficult. Many will physically resist being apprehended and can hurt or endanger the life of a Bounty Hunter. Many Bounty Hunters carry firearms.

Sell Merchandise

If you need to generate income, one way is to sell something. Salespeople are some of the most financially successful people in the world. You may not picture yourself as a salesperson, but you may be able to generate some significant additional income selling some things.

The good thing is you do not need to have the persuasive personality often associated with sales people to succeed at this. In fact, some people who do not have a friendly personality have used some of these methods to earn significant income.

What can you sell? The answer is very simple, you can sell anything people are willing to buy. And you may be surprised what people buy. There is an old saying, *one man's trash is another man's treasure.*

Go to a Flea Market and get an idea of some of the things people buy and sell.

37. Get Things for Free & Resell Them.

Some people make significant money getting things free and reselling them.

Many people want to get rid of things they no longer need or value. I have been surprised to learn, many times, there are people who want those items.

You may find good valuable items to resell, but you can also make money finding and selling smaller low-ticket items. I knew a man whose main income came from buying and reselling low-cost items. He told me he made the most money selling things for $1-2, which he got free or for 25 cents.

Consider this, if you pay $100 for an item and resell it for $150 you made a nice profit, but you have to find someone willing to pay the $150. What if you collect 100 small things for free and sell them for $2 each? More people are willing to spend $2 and you make more money if you sell all 100 items, which is very possible at a Flea Market.

If you plan to procure items and resell them, it can be very helpful to get a van, mini-van, or old school bus.

Some Places to Procure Free Things:

Freecycle

Join your local *Freecycle* group. Everything listed on there is free.

You may wonder how will you be able to sell something someone is giving away for free? Many people who give away things on *Freecycle* do not want to bother having a *Tag Sale* or do not want to try to sell the items on *eBay* or *Craigslist*. You can get those items free and resell them.

I received many things free on *Freecycle*, some of those things were worth a lot of money. Some of the homes where I picked up items from *Freecycle* were so remote no one would ever go there for a *Tag Sale*.

The limitation with *Freecycle* is you can only list or view items located within the *limited geographic area* of your *Freecycle* group. You cannot join a *Freecycle* group in another area.

Some people who list items on *Freecycle* only want to give items to people who need them. Others do not care who receives them. Always be honest. Do not tell people you want an item for yourself when you intend to resell it.

Craigslist

Many people list free items on *Craigslist*. The advantage with *Craigslist* is, unlike *Freecycle*, you are not limited to looking at listings only from your area. You can search listing from any geographic area.

Look at *Craigslist* frequently. People claim the good free items quickly.

If you find an item which interests you, respond right away and tell them you will take the item and will come pick it up as soon as possible.

Many people interested in an item request more pictures or information from the person offering it. If you make such a request that will put you further down on the list of people who *may* get the item. An item is listed free because they want someone to take it away as soon as possible. Contact the person who posted the item and offer to take it sight unseen.

Dumps/Recycling Centers

Municipal dumps or recycling centers can be a good source to find items you can resell.

Many times, people throw away good items. That often happens when people move.

You may find some valuable items which need minor repairs. I found many great items this way.

Many people bring boxes of things they did not sell at their *Tag Sale* to the dump right after their sale. Monday's or Saturdays are good days to go to the dump, if they are open.

Some dumps have areas where people can leave things for others to take. Some do not allow that.

Tag Sales

Some people have *Tag Sales* to try to make money. Most people have *Tag Sales* to get rid of things they no longer want. I have been to *Tag Sales* at the end of the day where people are glad to give away items, so they do not have to take them back inside.

Thrift Shops

Some people go to *Thrift Shops* and buy items at a low price and then re-sell them. Keep in mind some *Thrift Shops* do not have good prices on many items. You must know the value of an item and the resell value to make money this way.

Thrift Shops in more affluent areas tend to have better merchandise. Some may be overpriced. We used to go to a Thrift Shop in Darien, Connecticut which was like shopping at a Boutique.

Try to negotiate the price of a higher-priced item at a *Thrift Shop*. Or ask for a better price or discount if you buy multiple items.

Going Out of Business Sales

When a *Going Out of Business Sale* comes to an end merchants are often left with a lot of merchandise they need to get rid of.

You can often procure that leftover merchandise for pennies on the dollar. Sometimes you can get it free. Sometimes they may pay you if you will take it and dispose of it for them.

Remember they need to get rid of the merchandise and do not want to pay to store it. Make sure you have a place to store the items until you can sell them.

Places to Resell Things:
Flea Markets

Some Flea Markets are excellent places to re-sell things. Especially ones in affluent neighborhoods. I had a friend who took his items to Flea Markets in New

York City because things sold for so much more there.

Most Flea Markets charge a fee for a certain size space. Use your space wisely. Make it look good, so it attracts customers but not too good.

Make sure you display your items well to sell them.

I knew a man whose brother went to *Tag Sales* on Fridays. Then, on Saturdays he took what he bought to a *Flea Market* to sell them. He said his brother made more money doing that than he received from his pension as an engineer.

Remember, people love to get a deal. Always price things reasonable but higher than the minimum you want. That allows you room to negotiate.

If people do not negotiate and are willing to pay your asking price you may make more money offering them another item for a reduced price.

Many people who sell at *Flea Markets*, set up their booth, then cover it with tarps and go look at the other booths for good buys. They then bring those items back to their own booths and resell them. You should consider doing the same.

Craigslist

You can sell almost anything on *Craigslist*. The nice thing about *Craigslist* is it does not cost you anything to list an item.

Many people buy items locally on *Craigslist*, rather than buying from *eBay* or other places where they have to pay shipping. They go pick up the items.

When you sell *items* on *Craigslist*, the safest policy is to only accept cash for payment. Do not take Money Orders. There are too many counterfeit Money Orders.

eBay

Many people make a living selling things on *eBay*. It is a good idea to get advice from someone else who uses *eBay* to learn how to make the most money.

Most items sold on *eBay* have to be shipped. That means you must pack them carefully and pay to ship them. Always include a reasonable charge to cover shipping and related supplies.

Some people list bigger items on *eBay* with the notice the buyer must arrange to pick them up.

Tag Sales

Some people resell items at periodic *Tag Sales*. Doing joint *Tag Sales* with others usually attracts more buyers. Some municipalities have zoning restrictions as to how many *Tag Sales* you may have a year.

Consignment Shops

You may be able to sell some items at Consignment Shops. Some Consignment Shops specialize in selling clothing which is like new. Many shops sell children's clothing. Some specialize in sporting goods and equipment.

Some will display and sell the items for you for a commission of 25-50%, depending on the selling price of the item. Some shops will buy items for a set price or for an in-store credit.

They usually do not guarantee items against breakage.

Antique or Collectible Shops

You may sell some items to Antique and Collectible shops. They usually pay half the price they think they can sell it for. Some may work on consignment.

Pawn Shops

Pawn Shops buy items from you or offer you a loan against the value of the item. The best way to deal with a *Pawn Shop* is to sell them an item.

Pawn Shops will usually offer you at least half of the price you ask for an item, even if it is worth much more.

People working in *Pawn Shops* are some of the shrewdest people to deal with. You must learn how to negotiate with them.

If you have an item worth $500 and are willing to take $250 for it, when they ask you how much you want you should say $500. They will tell you why they cannot give you that and may offer you $250 or even $100. Whatever their first offer is they will usually pay at least 50 percent more than that. If you ask $250 for the $500 item, they will probably only offer you $100. They will not come up much more than to $125 or $150.

Selected Buyers

I know a woman who spent the entire $100 her husband gave her that week for family groceries at some *Tag Sales*. She then took some of the items she purchased to an interior decorator, who she previously hired to decorate her house, and sold some of the items to her for $200. After that, she went and bought $100 of groceries and used the $100 profit to continue her buying and reselling.

38. Offer to Clean Out Basements or Attics

This is a very good way to earn some money and probably get some things to resell. Many people will pay to get people to take away things which are cluttering their basements or attics. Some of those items will go directly to the dump but some can be resold.

Someone I knew advertised that he cleaned out attics. One time the owner of a house showed him their attic full of stuff and asked him for his price. He thought he could make a significant amount of money buying and reselling that lot, so he said $2,000. In his mind, that was the amount he was willing to pay. He was surprised with the owner gave him a check for $2,000 to take away the items. He then went and resold those items for almost $4,000.

39. Do Curbside Collection.

In many municipalities, people place their trash and unwanted items on the curb to be picked up. You may be amazed what people throw away.

Some municipalities prohibit people to collect those items, but many communities have no restrictions and welcome people taking items, as long as they do not make a mess or damage any property. They like the fact that makes less items end up in their landfill.

When I lived in Endicott, New York, I had a friend named Don who went out the night before the weekly garbage pick-up and collected items people were throwing away. He found furniture, tools, building supplies, bicycles, and toys. He invited me to go with him. We had a fun time together and found some great things.

Another time, I was at a speaking engagement in New Jersey. My friend, Frank asked if I would stay overnight and help him drop off his car at his mechanic in the morning. On the way to the mechanic I noticed huge piles of items along the side of every street. I asked what that was. He said every few years their town provided a day when you could put whatever you did not want out on the curb. People could then come by and take what they wanted, then the town disposed of what was left.

I was amazed at the quality and quantity of what people put on the curb. I found a nice children's desk, lawn furniture and more.

You may want to consider doing curbside collection and resell items you find. Even if you only sell a few items, it can mean some immediate extra income. Some people earn a living do that.

I knew a man who ran a garbage business in New Hampshire. He said he furnished his home and hunting camp with items he picked up by the side of the road. He told me he took many items to Thrift Shops and Antique Stores and resold them. He eventually sold his business for $1 million dollars.

40. Find & Sell Memorabilia.

Many people collect memorabilia. Some memorabilia is easily and inexpensively obtained at thrift shops, garage sales, and estate sales.

Consumable items people normally throw away, such as tickets, brochures and posters can generate some significant income.

The better condition an item is in, the higher the value. Unlike some other items, some memorabilia in poor condition can still be valuable if it is rare.

Travel Memorabilia

Travel memorabilia are items which feature the name of a certain location or place of interest. Some more common items are spoons, glasses, shirts, and hats.

Many people collect travel memorabilia. Some do it to remember trips they took. Some do it because they like certain places.

There is a wide variety of travel memorabilia. I have seen many of these items for sale for very low prices in thrift shops and at garage sales. With some creativity and good marketing, you may be able to buy and sell those items for a handsome profit.

One of the most overlooked area of travel memorabilia are maps, tickets, and brochures. They are often discarded. Items people normally discard tend to become more valuable. An original 1950's Disneyland Tourist Map sold for $5,500.

Event Memorabilia

Many people collect memorabilia from events such as concerts, theatres, conventions, and fairs. That includes tickets, posters, commemorative coins, event passes and pins.

Some old concert ticket stubs sell for hundreds of dollars. Some posters sell for thousands.

Political Memorabilia

Many people collect old political memorabilia. That includes posters, fliers, stickers, pins, banners, dolls, press passes, and correspondence from candidates. These can sell for a few dollars to thousands.

Sports Memorabilia

Many people collect sports memorabilia for their favorite team. Almost anything with a team logo can have value to some collector.

Look for tickets to old games, stadium maps, brochures, press kits, pins, and banners. Some old World Series tickets have sold for thousands of dollars.

I sold some team banners for hundreds of dollars.

Old Newspapers and Magazines

Some old newspapers and magazines can generate a significant amount of income. Ones which feature prominent events or people usually sell for more. Some have sold for thousands of dollars.

I know people who find old magazines, cut out the advertisements and sell those.

One time a lady walked into a shop owned by a friend of mine named Brian and saw he sold some old magazines. She told him her husband passed away and she was getting rid of bundles of old magazines he kept. She said she put a bundle out each week with the garbage but would gladly bring the remaining ones to him. When she returned he opened the first bundle and began to look through the magazines. He was surprised when he found a $20 bill inside of the first one. He was even more surprised when he found a $20 bill in the second one and then in every other issue.

Brian is one of the most ethical people I have ever met. He told the woman about his discovery. She was shocked. Every magazine in every stack had a $20 bill inside. She figured how many bundles of those magazine she put in the trash and realized she must have thrown away about $10,000.

Old Sheet Music

Some people collect old sheet music for different reasons. Some just like to play the music. Some collect it because some of it is valuable like other old documents. One of the more popular reasons old sheet music is collected is for decorating. Some of the most popular pieces feature images of entertainers.

Old Record Albums

Some people collect albums to listen to them. Some collect them as display pieces.

Many albums were issued in more than one run. The production information is often etched around the inner circle of the record and greatly affects their value.

Though it is good to find an old record and its cover, some people use old record album covers are decorations.

Old Photographs

Some old photographs can be worth a significant amount of money.

Years ago, a woman working at a magazine recovered old photographic prints from the dumpster outside of the magazine. After she died, her children found the photographs and noticed some prominent people featured in those photographs. They discovered the photographs were very valuable. They sold 21 of them at auction for $200 thousand.

41. Collect & Sell Items of Local Interest.

This method involves looking around for things which people where you live often take for granted, but which those outside of your area may like.

Some examples are items with the pictures or names of your town on them, or of other places in your area.

I have often seen items like this in local thrift shops selling inexpensively yet selling online for much more.

42. Sell Books.

Though more people read digital books than printed books, there are still many people who read printed books.

Many people read a book once and then do not keep it. That enables you to purchase some books for very low prices and resell them. A number of people earn their living doing this.

The best sources I found for acquiring these are at library book sales, garage sales, and some thrift shops. I have also found some valuable books at those venues.

There are now apps you can get for a smartphone which allow you to scan the barcode on a book to see what price it is currently selling for. Be careful, I encountered dishonest booksellers who list low sale prices for some books on their websites, books which they do not own, just to drive down the price of books when they try to buy them.

One of the challenges is to resell your books for the best profit. One problem is you must ship them. The shipping can cost more than the book itself. Many people who sell on-line combine items they sell to reduce shipping costs, customers really like that.

Two of the most popular places to sell books in on *eBay* or as an *Amazon.com* seller. You will find a lot of competition for common books on *Amazon*, so you will need to make very attractive listings.

Some books are in high demand and will sell well.

You could generate additional income advertising yourself as a Book Finder. Have people contact you with books they want. You then find the books for them and charge a flat rate or percentage for your service.

43. Sell Postcards.

For more than 100 years people have collected postcards both old and new. Some can be purchased inexpensively and sold for a significant profit.

There are many varieties of postcards. Some are quite simple, and some are very elaborate.

Some of the most popular postcards are ones of tourist attractions, local historic sites, waterfalls, landmarks, and scenic sites. There are also ones for special occasions and ones with romantic messages.

In 1873 the *United States Postal Service* started to print its own postal cards with postage on them.

Postcards from 1893 to 1920 are referred to as *Golden Age Postcards* and are highly desirable. Many of them were black and white images sent to Germany to be hand-colored.

Some people think unused postcards are more valuable. However, used postcards with old postage can often be the most valuable.

You can look for postcards at Tag Sales and Flea Markets. You will tend to get a better price at Tag Sales. You should consider posting on *Freecycle* or *Craigslist* that you are looking for old postcards.

44. Sell or Rent Vintage Clothing.

Vintage clothing are garments from a previous era. Vintage clothing always seems to have some resale value. Some people like to wear them. Some are used as costumes and are rented by theatres and film productions.

You can find these at Estate Sales, Flea Markets and Thrift Shops.

You need to be aware some insects like to eat old clothing, especially wool, mohair, fur, and feathers. Some of them are hard to see and spread from an infected garment to others.

The eight worst culprits are: *Carpet Beetle* (love natural fibers, especially wool); *Case Bearing Clothes Moth* (love fur, flannel and hair); *Cockroach* (love perspiration); *Cricket* (love food particles on clothing and laundry starch); *Firebrat* (especially like cotton, linen and rayon); *Silverfish* (love cotton and silk); *Termites* (goes after food particles on clothing or in pockets); and *Webbing Clothes Moth* (love wool and mohair).

Many of those insects lay eggs in clothing and keep reproducing. It is the larvae of the moths, not the adults, which do the damage.

You can use insecticides to kill the insects. I prefer organic methods. One effective method is to put garments in a freezer for at least 72 hours. Then dry clean and store them away from possibly infested garments.

45. Sell Home Décor.

Many people like to decorate their homes. Items you decorate with are called *Home Décor*. There is a vast host of items which fall under this category. Some are functional, many are just decorative.

Look in home decorating magazines or online for ideas of things people decorate with.

I have seen people decorate with old doors, bicycles, guns, industrial equipment, dried flowers, pictures, rugs, lamps, toys, coffee cans, barbed wire, figurines, coins, old sheet music, memorabilia, old clothing and much more.

You can find items which can be used as décor almost anywhere, from the dump to elite shops. Flea Markets, Tag Sales, and Thrift Shops are often good places to find bargains and good places to sell the items.

There is such a wide variety of items used as décor you may want to specialize in certain types.

Try to establish a relationship with some decorators who may become your preferred buyers. Give them first choice when you secure items.

You never know what you will find when you look for décor. A reenactor friend of mine, named Gary, was at a garage sale one day and saw a hat which people used for a decoration. He recognized it as Revolutionary War Dragoon style hat. He figured it was a reproduction and bought it. It turned out to be an original. He turned around and sold it for a few thousand dollars.

Another time he was at garage sale and saw a picture frame he liked. It had a painting in it which he did not care for, but he liked the frame and bought it for a few dollars. He later removed the painting and found one of the earliest original printed copies of the *Declaration of*

Independence. He sold that for many thousands of dollars.

He was then at a sale and bought an old trunk. In the trunk he found an old flag. He discovered the trunk belonged to a colonel of the local militia. He had it appraised and found it was the oldest numbered Pre-Revolutionary War Regimental flag found in America. It is called the *Southold Militia Pine Tree Flag*. He had it appraised and was told it was worth $500,000. He put it in a special frame to preserve it. He brought it to a reenactment and showed it to me. It was amazing. A few years later, after *Sotheby's* sold the *Tarleton Flags*, the value of his flag increased to more than $2 million.

46. Sell Trading Cards.

Trading cards have been made for more than 100 years for a variety of subjects. Some of the first trading cards featured baseball players and were sold with tobacco. They were soon followed by trading cards sold with candy.

Some early cards now sell for thousands of dollars. You must be careful because many of them were counterfeited.

Over the years trading cards expanded to include more sports. Then another popular category developed known as *Non-Sports Cards*. Non-Sports Cards include: musicians; actors; movies; television shows; comic characters; and much more.

Superman Trading cards from the 1940's sell for $300 to $400 each. A much more recent card from the *Pokémon* Series sold for $20,000.

In 1962 *Topps* made two non-sports card sets with some very graphic images called: *Civil War News* and *Mars Attacks*. The *Civil War News* set now sells for hundreds of dollars. The *Mars Attack* set sells for thousands of dollars.

In 1964 *Topps* made a set featuring a new music group called *The Beatles*. That set sells for more than $1,000.

You can generate additional income selling trading cards, but you must follow some careful guidelines.

Selling trading cards is a market that fluctuates greatly. Be careful about speculating in this field. There was a big boom in the 1980's that crashed overnight in the 1990's. Many people speculated and lost lots of money. Back then I had a card which was worth $300 on a Friday. I had a buyer lined up to pick up the card on Monday. The trading card market crashed that weekend and the card's value dropped to $10 by Monday.

You may want to keep some cards as a possible future investment. Sports rookie cards, team sets, special insert cards have shown a historical price increase.

One good piece of advice I was given regarding trading cards is to only buy ones you like. One reason for that is you may end up stuck with the cards.

If you buy current cards because you like them and find ones which have a high value, you may want to consider selling them right away if you want to make money.

You will find many older trading cards for sale very inexpensively. They often have very little value. The exception to that is if the person selling them was not a collector and just happened to buy the cards new and held on to them. If other people have not sorted through the cards you may find some valuable cards. That is especially true of baseball cards. For example, most baseball cards from 1984 have very little value but a Don Mattingly rookie card could be worth hundreds of dollars.

Some people collect cards which feature their favorite team, athlete, or celebrity. Sometimes I look through a box of old assorted cards and pick out key players and ones from one or two teams to use as gifts or to possibly resell.

The condition of a trading card drastically effects the value. It can make the price differ from hundreds to thousands of dollars. The difference between the different grads of cards is miniscule. Handle all cards with care.

This is one field where I will only buy cards in person. I will never buy cards online expecting to resell them.

47. Sell Stamps.

Stamp collecting is a very old hobby, one followed by young and old alike. It is one which can generate significant income, if you approach it wisely.

Some stamps sell for pennies, yet some sell for millions of dollars. You may be able to find some valuable ones if you know what to look for.

When I was a youth we used to cut off stamps and their cancellations from envelopes. They were then donated and used to help fund a home for orphans in Norway. The orphanage resold them (the stamps, not the orphans) to international stamp collectors. Those stamps had little value in my country but generated income in Norway.

As with many other items the condition of a stamp greatly effects its value. Usually unused stamps have the highest value but there are exceptions. In 2009 an envelope with a rare stamp featuring Abraham Lincoln, which was mailed in 1873, sold for $431,000. That was a unique find, but there are other valuable finds out there. You just need to know what to look for.

I was involved with a transaction which included a few envelopes with cancelled stamps mailed from occupied France which sold for a few thousand dollars.

It is interesting to note some very valuable stamps are stamps printed with errors which were later corrected. In 1918, the United States Postal Service printed a stamp featuring a Curtis JN-4 airplane. By mistake, they printed 100 copies upside down. It is called the *Inverted Jenny*. One of those sold for more than $1 million.

If you get tired collecting stamps and have old U.S. Postal Stamps they can always be used for their face value for mailing letters.

48. Sell Collectables.

There are hundreds of different types of collectables people are willing to buy. What is a collectable? A collectable is anything people collect.

Go to a Flea Market and look around to get an idea of what people sell. You will probably be surprised. People sell both old and new things. Many things they sell I would have thrown away. Identify things which interest you. You will usually do best selling things which interest you.

Just a few types of items people collect are: tools, dolls, furniture, instruments, dishes, cups, records, cameras, clothing, shoes, hats, art, pens, razors, fishing rods, fishing lures, toys, photographs, records, old cameras, maps, rugs, old sports equipment, sports memorabilia, autographs, bicycles, cars, car parts, calendars, eye glasses, knives, old bottles, jewelry, watches, combs, matchboxes, and figurines.

You can find collectables at Flea Markets, Garage Sales, Tag Sales, Thrift Shops, at the dump, along the curb, or in an attic or basement.

There are many places to sell collectables. You can sell them at Flea Markets, Garage Sales, Tag Sales, on *eBay*, on *Craigslist* and on other online sites.

I recommend you try to look up the value of an item before you try to sell it. It may not sell for that price but knowing that information will help you negotiate better.

49. Find & Sell Used Pianos.

Selling used pianos is a good way to make some money. There are a number of people who would like a piano in their home as a decoration and others who want one so someone in the family can play or learn to play.

Years ago, many homes had a piano and many people took piano lessons. As the years passed, fewer and fewer people took piano lessons. Some who took lessons, lost interest and the piano was no longer used.

Pianos are a large heavy piece of furniture, so they often stay in the same room. Pianos are expensive to move so they are often left behind.

Because of a combination of those factors, many people

have pianos they no longer want. Many are in excellent condition. If you can pick them up, you can often get used pianos for free.

Understand there are six different types of pianos.

Grand Piano *(6'-10' long) (800-1200 lbs.)*

These are often seen in concert halls and parlors. These require a lot of room. They usually have a beautiful sound. These are great for decorating. They can sell for a lot of money.

Baby Grand Piano *(4'-6"-6'6"long) (500-800 lbs.)*

These are beautiful smaller versions of the Grand Piano. These fit in more homes and are great decorator pieces.

Square Grand Piano *(750-830 lbs.)*

There are large rectangular pianos from the 1800s. These are not very common, but you will still find people who have them and want to get rid of them. They have a gentler tone than modern pianos. They require different tools to tune them. They often have a cracked sounding board, which you probably cannot fix. Some people will pay you to take these away. These can be great decorator pieces.

Upright Piano *(500-900 lbs.)*

Also called an Upright Grand. These are tall. These can have a nice full sound. These are very common and frequently offered for free.

Player Pianos *(900 lbs.)*

These are Upright Pianos with a mechanism which uses perforated scrolls to play specific songs. You can also play these like a regular piano. Often the player portion does not work. If it does, and you can get some rolls of music. These can be resold easier than some of the other models.

Spinet Piano *(300-500 lbs.)*

These are the shorter cousins to the Upright Pianos.

These are more popular for reselling because they fit easier in homes and apartments. They are much easier to move than any of the others.

Method I Used Many Times to Get a Free Piano:

☐ Make sure you have a vehicle or trailer which can hold the piano. You can rent a small moving truck from *U-Haul* or *Home Depot*.

☐ Enlist people to help move it. You may be able to move a spinet piano with two strong people, but you need more help to move other models. I recommend four people, or two gorillas. ☺

☐ Put an ad in a local classified paper or on *Craigslist* or *Freecycle* stating you want a free piano. You may be surprised how many offers you receive. I used classified ads a number of times in both urban, suburban, and rural areas and received many offers for free pianos.

☐ Ask for a complete description. Ask for the model and condition. Ask if all the keys work and if they know the last time, it was tuned.

☐ Ask where it is located. Is it upstairs? We found a nice piano on a second floor. We determined there was no way to get it down those stairs. They originally hoisted it up from the outside into the apartment. Years ago, they remodeled the apartment so there was no way to get it out without dismantling it.

50. Sell Hides.

You can generate significant income selling hides. I had a friend named Morgan who put his children through Ivy League Colleges with the money he earned selling hides.

If you live in an area where people hunt, you will find many hunters hunt for meat. Some may keep the head of the game to mount (which is very expensive) or they may save the antlers, but many do nothing with the hide.

When I was in college, I was not a hunter but had friends who were. One of my classmates said he collected hides during hunting season and traded them with a tanner for tanned deer hides (which are expensive). I asked him if I got some hides if I could also trade some in. He agreed, and we gathered a large load of hides to take to the tanner. The only drawback was I had to keep the hides in the trunk of my car for a week. They had a less than desirous odor. We then took the load to the tanner and came away with about $300 worth of tanned deerskin.

You can make crafts and clothing with the tanned hides or you can just resell them.

If you do not know any hunters you can place a free ad on *Craigslist* saying you will pick up hides.

Another good source for free hides is Roadkill. I have a section in my book, *More Than 200 Extreme Ways to Reduce Expenses*, on finding and harvesting Roadkill. Here is some relevant information from that book, which you can apply for harvesting roadkill for hides.

Roadkill is a dead animal you find on or near the road, which was killed by a vehicle. Though the idea of collecting and eating roadkill or taking their hides is repulsive to some, some call it an *act of respect* to the animal. They say it honors an animal when you utilize its meat or hide and do not waste its tragic death.

The *National Highway Administration* estimates one million animals are killed on U.S. roads *every day*. Thousands are killed every day in Europe and Australia. More than half of the panthers killed in Florida every year are killed by cars.

In 1993, twenty-five different schools worked together on a project to determine roadkill statistics in America. They came up with the following annual Roadkill statistics, most of which were still accepted as the national average some 20 years later:
- 41 million squirrels
- 22 million rats
- 19 million opossums
- 15 million raccoons
- 350,000 deer

The figure for deer is much lower than the 1.5 million now reported by the *National Highway Administration*.

If an animal has an intimate encounter with a truck, there may not be much meat to salvage. However, frequently there is little damage to the hide.

Harvesting and eating roadkill or keeping the hides is legal in most states. Laws change rapidly so check your local laws before harvesting. The laws cited here were current when this book was written.

Some states like Massachusetts and Pennsylvania do not have any laws related to roadkill. Some states have very specific laws regulating the collection or possession of roadkill.

It is illegal to harvest any roadkill in some states like California, Tennessee, and Washington. Nevada does not have any laws about harvesting roadkill but has prosecuted people who do that as poachers.

Some State Regulations about Roadkill:

Alaska - Moose is state property. You may not harvest any dead moose. The state donates any moose killed on a road to charitable groups.

Connecticut – If you hit an animal and kill it, you may keep it. If you do not keep it, anyone may take it.

Florida – If you hit it, you can keep it.

Georgia - You can keep a deer but not a bear.

Illinois - The driver who hits a deer may claim it but must take it at the scene of the accident and only during deer season.

Montana – If you hit and kill a deer, moose, elk, or antelope, you may keep them. You may not keep a bear, mountain lion or *Bighorn Sheep*.

New Jersey – Requires a permit to harvest roadkill.

New York – You are allowed to keep deer, moose or bear you hit and kill, but must file a report.

Oregon – You may gather dead coyote, skunks,

badgers, opossum, porcupines, and weasel without permission. No one, except those with a furbearer license are allowed to collect deer, elk, bear, or raccoon killed along the road unless given specific permission from State Police or State Wildlife officials.

Texas - Lawmakers passed a resolution *discouraging* harvesting roadkill, not prohibiting it.

Vermont – If you hit a beaver you can keep it, but you must report any deer you hit.

51. Sell Animal Horns.

Some people like animal horns. You may be able to generate additional income selling animal horns or crafts made from them.

Horns and antlers are different. Many people mistakenly refer to antlers as horns.

Antlers grow on the male members of *Cervidae family*, which includes all species of deer, moose, and elk, as well on an occasional rare Jackalope. Antlers are shed each year and new larger ones grow back.

Horns are found on members of the *Bovidae family*, which includes cows, goats, sheet, gazelles, and antelopes.

Both the males and females of some species grow horns. Horns do not branch out and do not shed. Horns continue to grow until the animal dies.

Horns from the *Texas Longhorn Cattle* are very popular. The bull's horns can grow to over 5 feet wide and the cow's horns to more than 8 feet wide. Mounted pairs of those horns can sell from $250 for small ones to more than $1,000 for large ones.

Some people make instruments from horns. Some people of the Orthodox Jewish faith blow a *shofar* on some holy days. The *shofars* are made from a ram's horn. Those can sell from $20 all the way up to thousands of dollars. To generate some additional income, you may want to consider making and selling *shofars*.

52. Sell Local Rocks, Sand, Water or Air.

There are people who collect and will pay for natural items with local interest. You might want to collect some of these things and sell them to those people.

Select a simple appropriate container, preferable a clear one, for your items. That will protect them and let people display them. You can use a small zip lock bag, but a simple clear pill-sized plastic container looks better.

Print a nice descriptive label, on your printer, for each item. Be sure to include the specific place the item is from, the date it was collected, and who collected it. Then sign or initial it to verify its authenticity.

Make sure there are no restrictions in place from removing items from a site.

Some places like the *Painted Desert, Petrified Forest*, National Battlefields or the *Great Wall of China*, forbid collection, or removal of any items.

Sometimes there is a way around the prohibition. I collected petrified wood along the road just outside the boundary of a National Park, where it was allowed. You can collect a soil sample adjacent to a battlefield.

If you go to the *Great Wall of China* there are some approved gift shops which sell pieces of the wall. You can buy those and break them into smaller pieces to resell.

Some Suggested Items to Sell:
Rocks or Minerals

Many people collect rocks and minerals. That is addressed in this book as another item, but this is about selling them as a local interest item, which is different. Some people want to have a rock or mineral from every state or from different countries.

Sand or Soil

Some people like to have sand or soil samples from various places of interest.

It is easy to collect sand from a beach or desert.

To collect soil from a place of interest, battlefield, or significant site you must be more careful. If permitted, it is best to use a hand spade to collect your sample instead of a big shovel or backhoe. Collect your sample from a place which does not damage or mar the location.

Water

Water samples are easy to collect. You only need a few ounces. Some examples people may ant are from an ocean, river, waterfall, or famous water fountain.

If collecting water from a waterfall it is best to collect your sample at the bottom of the waterfall instead of trying to collect some as you fall over the top of the falls.

Air

A novelty item is to collect air from different places. These are sometimes listed on *eBay*.

Air for sale is usually placed in clear bottles with labels identifying where and when they were collected.

Items from popular or historically significant places will probably be worth more.

To stir your imagination, the following are some possible locations to collect air: Wall Street; Times Square; Niagara Falls; The Rocky Mountains; Thomas Jefferson's Monticello; Buckingham Palace; a pine forest; or a beach.

Be careful if you collect air in Washington, D.C., the air can be real toxic there at times.

53. Sell Things for Other People.

Many people have things they would like to sell but do not want to go through all the details required for selling and shipping items. That creates an opportunity for you to sell things for other people.

You can generate additional income if you take care of all the details of selling an item. Your job is to sell the items and make sure the buyer receives them. You either pick up the items or have people bring the items to you.

Two Basic Ways You Can Get Paid:
☐ Pay the Seller a Set Price When Items Sell.

☐ Get Paid a Percentage. You can either sell the items for a percentage of the sale or sell them on consignment. It is usually best to work out an arrangement where you get paid a percentage of the sales price.

A Few Ways to Sell These Things:
☐ Sell the Things Online
☐ Be an *eBay* Reseller.
☐ Sell Things on *Craigslist*.
☐ Sell Through Regional Tag Sales Sites.
☐ Conduct an Estate Sale or Tag Sale for People.
☐ Take Items to Consignment Shops.
☐ Try to Sell the Items at a Flea Market.

You must be prepared to let the seller know how much an item is worth and how much you think you can sell it for. An item could be worth $100 but may only sell for $50 in the current market. You agree to get a percentage of the sale price. That is usually somewhere between 20 to 40 percent.

Getting paid a percentage of the sale price is an incentive for you to sell the item at a higher price.

If you are selling items on an auction site like *eBay*, you have the option of setting a *Buy It Now Price* or you can list it for auction. If you list it for auction, it is a good idea to set a *Reserve Price* (the minimum bid you will accept).

Consider the following example. Someone may have a Commemorative World Series Banner which you determine is worth $100. You and the seller agree they will be happy if they get $50. That means if your fee is 25%, it must sell for $62 for them to get $51. You can list it with a *Buy It Now* price of $62. If it sells for that, they get $51 and you get $17. Or, you can put it up for auction with a starting bid of $10, with a $62 Reserve. If the highest bid is $61, it will not sell. If the bid is $62 or higher, that is what it will sell for, plus the shipping fee. If it sells for more than $62 you both make more money.

You must keep in mind that *eBay* allows some buyers to return items, so it is wise not to let the payer know this and that they will not be paid until a specified time period after the sale.

Make Money with Things You Make

Many people generate income making and selling crafts and other things they make. You may not consider yourself a crafty person, but you may be surprised to discover you can make things other people will buy. You just need a good idea and a place to sell what you make.

I never thought I would make money sewing things. I never sewed a day in my life until I started reenacting. I learned to hand sew authentic historical reproductions. One day I started to sell and rent some of the garments and accoutrements I made.

54. Do Needlework.

Many people like handmade items. People produce some very nice desirable items with needlework. The three most popular methods of needlework are: knitting, crocheting, and embroidering.

You need to learn some skills to do needlework, but most people can learn them quickly.

You can create your own designs and items or do custom work. Never use copyrighted patterns which state you may not re-sell the items you make.

My daughter Grace crochets amazing projects. Over the years she made beautiful gifts. People tell her she could sell her items for good money.

Some people make additional income with needlework by raising sheep or alpacas for yarn. I knew a lady who raised alpacas and sent the wool to someone else to process for her. It cost her more than $300 to have someone else process the wool and make the yarn. You will generate even more income if you process the yarn.

55. Do Weaving.

Woven items can sell for a lot of money. There are not many people who weave, so you may be able to fill a niche and generate some good money.

There are many different types of weaving. Some people weave fabric, some wave rugs, tapestries, belts and much more.

Weaving usually requires some kind of loom. Some looms fit in your lap while some are like large pieces of furniture.

If you want to do some weaving which is more profitable, you may want to consider weaving historical reproductions. Very few people do that, and historically accurate reproductions sell for a lot of money.

56. Make Quilts.

If you have a lot of time on your hands you may want to consider making and selling quilts. Quilts are wonderful decorative and functional items which usually take about 100 hours to make. That is one reason they can sell for a significant amount of money.

I have a friend Calvin, whose brother made and sold quilts for hundreds of dollars while serving in the military.

Quilts are either handsewn or made with a machine. Some use a combination of the two methods. Hand sewing quilts is less expensive to do because you do not need a sewing machine or the cost of electricity to power one.

Many quilts are made with blocks or strips of material. Some are very basic and made simply by sewing together scraps of material. Some quilts are very elaborate with carefully planned designs. Some have intricate hand-stitched designs. The more elaborate the handicraft the higher the price of the quilt.

57. Do Beadwork.

Many people like beadwork. You may be able to learn how to do beadwork and earn some extra income.

When my father was in high school, he spent some summers living with some members of the Mohawk tribe. Years later, I married a girl with Mohawk ancestry. While staying with the tribe one of the things my father learned was how to do beadwork. He made bracelets and elaborate costumes which I treasure to this day.

My father taught me how to do bead work using what are called *seed beads*. They are very small and can make beautiful designs.

When I was a teen I discovered many girls liked necklaces and bracelets. If I wanted to get to know a girl better, I would make her a handmade beaded one.

It is not hard to learn to do beadwork. The supplies are relatively inexpensive. You need a loom, beads, thread, needles, backing material, and clasps for some projects.

You can make and sell necklaces, bracelets, and other beadwork. You can also add beadwork to vests, moccasins, handbags, and other garments for greater profit.

Never use copyrighted patterns and designs.

Even though you may do beadwork with tribal-like designs, never claim what you make is tribal beadwork unless you are a member of a tribe. You can call them as tribal reproductions. If you call them tribal reproductions, I recommend you donate a percentage of your profits to helping some tribal heritage programs.

If you want to become a member of a tribe you can join the *Wannabe Tribe* on *Facebook*. Then you can say your beadwork was made by a member of the *Wannabe Tribe*.

58. Do Simple Sewing Repairs.

Many people need simple sewing repairs but do not know how to do them. You can generate extra income if you learn some basic sewing repair skills.

Replacing Buttons

Many people lose buttons on their garments and need them replaced but do not know how to do that.

Use thread the same color as the thread used to attach the buttons which are intact. I usually use silk thread which is very thin but very strong.

Patching Holes & Tears

When I was younger we used to sew patches on our jeans if they became torn. Now that torn jeans are a fashion statement maybe you should sell your torn jeans instead of patching them.

If you plan to patch holes or tears they are a little harder to fix, especially if it is in a prominent location.

59. Do Simple Alterations.

Some people have garments they need altered. Some alterations are quite simple, while others are complex. You may be able to learn the necessary skills to generate income doing alterations.

Some Simple Alterations You Might Offer.

Adjusting Length

There are times people need the length of a garment adjusted. Making a garment shorter is much easier than making one longer.

When I make a garment shorter I fold up fabric inside, where it cannot be seen, rather than cut it off. That way the garment can be made longer again if needed.

Making Loose Garments Fit Better

You can usually make a loose garment fit but may not be able to make one fit that is too tight, unless it has extra material.

When adjusting the fit of a garment, I highly recommend retaining as much fabric as possible instead of cutting it off.

The width of a garment can often be reduced by making small folds in the material, known as *pleats*. Sometimes one pleat in the back of a shirt, dress or pants is all that is needed. Sometimes it may take two or three pleats.

Sleeves which are too loose can often be folded in along the seams to fit better.

60. Do Custom Sewing.

You may be able to learn how to sew and make your own clothing or make clothing for others. That clothing can look as good or better than what they buy in a store. Properly made custom clothing will often fit better and look better.

You may wonder, how can I sew as good a garment as those sold in a shop? Just remember all clothing is sewn by someone. The person who sewed the garment may have mass produced it on a machine in North Carolina or perhaps in China or Thailand. Perhaps it was custom sewn in some dress or tailor shop or was sewn by a relative.

Some of the factors which make one garment cost more than others are often subjective.

One of the most important elements is how well does a garment fit and how good does it look on a person.

Many affluent people often pay to have their clothing custom made because it is fitted specifically for them and that makes them look better.

When I was in college the pastor of the church I attended was recognized by businessmen in the area as *the Best Dressed Man in Town*. Many of the men who gave him that honor wore suits which cost hundreds of dollars. The interesting thing was, unknow to them, his wife made all of his clothes.

If you learn how to sew and do good custom-fitted clothing you may be able to make a nice profit doing that.

61. Make, Sell or Rent Costumes.

Many people like to dress up in costumes. Some reports say adults spend more money on Halloween than any other holiday. Many people also dress up for *Steampunk, Cosplay, Comicon* and *Renaissance Fairs*.

At Halloween time there are many stores which open for one or two months to sell Halloween Costumes. Some of those costumes sell for hundreds of dollars.

There are always shops selling or renting clothing for *Renaissance Fairs, Steampunk* or *Cosplay* events. That clothing sells for a premium price. You may be able to generate income making costumes and then selling or renting them for those types of events.

Local Theatre's are a good place which need costumes.

Costumes should look historically correct but do not need to be to the same standard as historically authentic reproductions used at historic sites or by reenactors.

62. Make Historical Clothing.

Making Historical Clothing falls under two categories: Historical Costumes and Historically Authentic Reproductions. I have made both types.

Historical Costumes

Historical Costumes are used by individuals for parties and other events. They are also used for stage and some film productions. These should look historically accurate (though often they do not) but do not necessarily have to be made of historically correct materials or constructed with historically correct techniques.

Historically Authentic Reproductions

Historically authentic reproductions should look

accurate. In the *Living History Guild,* we classify reproductions as either Apprentice, Journeyman or Craftsman. All of them must be researched to look like authentic period clothing. These can sell for good money online or at reenactments.

☐ **Apprentice** – These items look good from six feet. They may not be made of the proper materials but that cannot be detected from six feet away. Garments which were historically handsewn, may be sewn on machine if that cannot be detected from six feet.

These garments are good for most characters in a film project and for many reenactors.

☐ **Journeyman** – These garments must look good up-close. The materials and techniques must appear historically correct. All visible seams must be sewn with period correct methods. Unseen seams and linings do not need to be done with historically correct techniques.

It must be understood, some historical handsewn garments are were done so well they look like they were machine sewn.

These garments are good for close up film projects and for most reenactors.

☐ **Craftsman** – These garments not only look good up-close but are constructed using only historically correct materials and construction. That includes all seams seen or unseen.

Some of the Craftsman regimental coats I make include handmade leather cords, which cannot be seen, which hold the buttons in place.

The price for historically accurate items varies according to the item and the level of authenticity. Sometimes you can buy an Apprentice level regimental coat online for as low as $300. You should expect to pay $600 or more for a Journeyman level regimental coat and a minimum of $1,200 to $2,500 for a Craftsman level regimental coat.

63. Make & Sell Dolls & Puppets.

There is always a market for dolls and puppets. They are loved by young and old alike.

There are many different ways to make dolls and puppets to sell.

Make Sock Puppets from Old Socks

It is easy to make sock puppets with little or no expense. Take a sock and slide it over your hand and you have an instant puppet.

You can draw on eyes or you can make eyes out of buttons, felt, old Ping-Pong balls or Styrofoam balls.

You can add value and character by dressing up your sock puppets many different ways.

My father worked with Shari Lewis. She was a famous puppeteer whose most famous puppet was named *Lambchop*. Lambchop was a type of sock puppet.

Make Sock Dolls from Old Socks

Years ago, people made dolls from socks. Use your imagination or find ideas on how to do this online.

You can draw eyes on the doll or use buttons for eyes or sew them on.

You can use white socks and make snowman dolls like *Olaf the Snowman*.

Make Stocking Dolls

Some people make dolls from stockings and give them away as gifts or sell them for extra income. Some of those, look nice, some look creepy. You can find simple instructions for making these online.

Make Rag Dolls

Rag dolls have been around for many years. They are relatively easy to make. The simplest method is to cut out two copies of a doll shape. You then sew them together around the outside edges, then turn that inside out and stuff it with rags or filling. You can make clothing from small scraps of materials. You can draw on eyes or use buttons or hand sew them on.

Make Wood Dolls or Puppets

You can make dolls or puppets from wood. Many antique dolls and puppets have wooden heads and rag or sock bodies.

Make Dolls from Kits

Some people buy kits and make dolls. Beware, my mother made dolls from kits but liked her creations too much to sell them.

Make Muppet-Type Puppets

For many years I travelled using high quality Muppet-type puppets my wife made. Most of them were made with foam and fabric. People often asked to buy them.

64. Make Doll Clothing.

For many years people have made money selling clothing for dolls. You will find a lot of expensive and inexpensive doll clothing available commercially.

If you want to make significant money with this method, the best thing is to design your own clothing and be very good at it.

You may want to design outfits which mimic popular full-sized designer outfits.

You will probably make the most money doing custom work. That can also save you money because you do not need to maintain an inventory.

65. Do Doll Repairs & Restoration.

You can provide a service repairing and restoring old dolls, or you can find old dolls to restore and resell.

You will probably make more money repairing and restoring dolls for other people. There are some people who would love to have their favorite old doll restored.

There are others who would love to have a someone's old doll restored as an especially meaningful present.

In the Disney film, *Toy Story II*, the main character Woody was damaged and then stolen. The man who stole him paid a specialist to restore Woody to like new condition, so he could get a higher price selling him to a museum. You could learn to do the same.

There are some skills you have to develop in order to undertake this method. The key is learning how to clean and restore a doll to like new condition.

One of the most common fixes dolls require is to restore their snarled hair. If the doll does not have real human hair, one of the ways to restore the hair is to wash it with fabric softener.

You can also make wigs for dolls. This can be done using human wigs or yarn. Some yarn can be used as is or can unwound to make even better wigs.

66. Make & Sell Doll Furniture.

There is a market for well-made doll furniture. I have a friend whose wife collects doll furniture. Some of her pieces she bought cost more than full-sized furniture.

If you make and resell doll furniture do not use commercial patterns if they stipulate you cannot resell items you make with their patterns.

Also make sure you do not use copyrighted character names for your furniture.

If you become good at this, you may be able to partner with a furniture store to see doll-sized reproductions of their furniture for their customers.

67. Make & Sell Wooden Items.

Many people like handcrafted wooden items. If you are a little handy you may be able to make items from wood to resell. Those items could be simple or elaborate. Many do not require great woodworking skills.

Do an online search for wooden items to make and you will get ideas for endless projects.

You could sell these at crafts sales, on-line, or to specialty shops.

You can buy wood for making items or you may be able to make some of them from scrap wood.

We had friends Dave and Emma in Danbury, Connecticut, who made and toys from scrap wood. Their Noah's Ark Toy Chest was a very popular item.

Toys

There are many wood toys you can make. Look online or at craft shows for ideas.

One year, I made riding stick animals for our children and wooden games another year. They are still around some 30 years later.

Furniture

Making your own furniture is a way to save a lot or money and also a way to make extra income.

My son Daniel did not have any wood working training, yet he made a variety of very nice wood furniture projects which look like they were store bought. He made bunk beds with study areas underneath them. He also made a long dining room table and sofas.

You can do this with power tools or can do it like they did it for thousands of years, using simple hand tools.

68. Do Toy Restoration.

If you like toys, this is one way to make some income. Many people throw away toys when they break. You should be able to fix some toys with a little glue or touch up paint. Sometimes all they need are new batteries.

You can do custom restoration, which is probably the most profitable, or you can go to thrift shops and tag sales and look for toys to restore.

If a toy has batteries which corroded inside, sometimes

they can be fixed. Remove the old batteries and then scrap out the corrosion. Then use fine sandpaper and clean off the connections.

Some toys use the small flat round batteries. I often get a number of those on a sheet at a Dollar Store.

69. Make & Sell Duck Calls.

I was surprised to learn more than 1 million people duck hunted in the 2016-2017 duck season. Many of those people use duck calls to help bring the ducks near them.

It is possible you could make good money making and selling duck calls. Phil Robertson, who was featured with his family on the television show, *Duck Dynasty*, discovered that and made millions of dollars.

70. Sell Scrimshaw.

Scrimshaw is often artwork or words carved on whale teeth, ivory, bones, tusks, piano keys, or shells.

People have been doing scrimshaw for thousands of years. Sailors and soldiers, with time on their hand, used to do elaborate scrimshaw carvings.

You can buy and resell scrimshaw but may be able to make more money if you made and sold your own.

One day a reenactor I know showed me one of the nicest pieces of scrimshaw I had ever seen. It was a powder horn carved with a scenic map of the Hudson Valley during the Revolutionary War. I asked him where he purchased such a fine piece. He surprised me when he told me he made it himself. I admired his artwork. He then told me that was the first piece of art work he ever did. Like him, you may discover you have hidden artistic talent.

You can make your own scrimshaw horns from scratch or buy kits for under $30. The finished product could sell for many times that amount.

Some people make significant money making and selling scrimshaw jewelry.

71. Make & Sell Memorial Displays.

Making Memorial Displays is a very meaningful way to generate income. Memorial Displays memorialize someone who is deceased or honors a past event. Many people would love to have a Memorial Display to remember a loved one. These can also be done for organizations or historical sites.

I was born in New York City. I will never forget watching the horror unfold on September 11, 2001, when terrorists hijacked four airplanes. They flew two of them into the *Twin Towers* in New York City and one into the Pentagon. The fourth plane was stopped by heroic passengers, who gave their lives to save others.

I went to *Ground Zero* shortly after the attack and had to cover my face as the smoke and clouds of dust covered the area for blocks. I stood on top of a building and picked up charred remains of papers which blew out of one of the planes and some others from the buildings which fell.

While there, I wrote a remembrance as I stood covered in debris, looking at the rescue effort. Afterwards, I made a Memorial Display of that event. I put a local afternoon newspaper from 9-11 in the frame as a background. I then placed the remembrance I wrote, plus some of the charred paper on top of the newspaper. I brought that display to various events to remind people of what happened that day. I was touched as I saw tears come to many eyes.

A nice way to make a Memorial Display is to make a shadowbox (use a deep picture frame). Select or make a nice background, then add pictures and some small items.

Here is a nice way to make a Memorial Display for an individual. Use an article of clothing the person wore for the background. Place a picture of the person in the middle. If you can find a picture of them wearing that article of clothing that is even better. Add various items, which belonged to the person, such as some jewelry they wore. You could add an old tool or kitchen utensil they used. You can also add some small items they collected. It is even more special if you can add something they wrote by hand, such as an old letter, postcard of recipe.

If you are making these for family members, you can cut out pieces of the same garment and use the same picture, or use a different garment and different picture, as well as different items for each person. These will be treasured for generations to come.

You can also make displays of a historical nature for historic sites, museums, schools, or local businesses. If you do this well, once people see your work, you will most likely have a steady stream of customers.

72. Make & Sell Memory Displays.

There is a difference between Memorial Displays and Memory Displays. Memorial Displays honor someone who is deceased or remember a past somber event. Memory Displays usually honor the living or more joyous events.

There are various themes you can use for Memory Displays such as: military service, weddings, births, birthdays, anniversaries, concerts, special recognition, vacations, sports teams, favorite players and more.

You can make these in various sizes and design as simple or complex as you want.

You could make a shadow box for a particular team with the team logo, stadium, or magazine cover as the backdrop. Then add team related memorabilia, trading cards, tickets, a hat, and pictures. You could also add an action figure or autograph of a player with the team.

73. Sell Fresh Flowers.

If you have space for a garden you may want to raise some flowers to sell. The amount of space you need to do this may be smaller than you think.

Some people in apartment complexes have tiered planters or small greenhouses on their porches or in rooms near windows. Some have gardens on rooftops. Some use fire escapes or community gardens.

I had a friend in New Hampshire with a small yard who made all his space count. He planted all around the outside of his house, along his fence, and around all the trees in his yard and had a great harvest every year.

If you have more space you can grow more.

According to *Headstart Publishing*, raising and selling cut flowers is one of the most profitable means of generating income from a small parcel of land. They say you can generate about $30,000 of income from one acre.

They claim the top 10 most profitable flowers people grow and sell are: *Ageratum, Scabiosa, Larkspur, Snapdragon, Peony, Zinnias, Sunflowers, Verbena Bonariensis, Salvia* and *Yarrow*.

You can sell flowers at farmers markets. Restaurants and hotels are also great outlets.

74. Deliver Flower Arrangements.

Some small florists need people to deliver their flower arrangements. It helps if you have a car, but some people do it on bicycle. Some who live in cities use mass transit.

You can usually earn more money if a florist has multiple deliveries which can be made to the same location, such as a hospital or office building.

You can make more money making your own flower arrangements which you make and deliver. They do not have to be made with live fresh flowers.

75. Place Flower Arrangements on Graves.

Some people like to honor their departed loved ones by placing flower on their graves but are unable to do this themselves. You can provide a very meaningful service and generate income at the same time by providing a service where you place arrangements on graves for birthdays, anniversaries, and holidays like: Valentines' Day,

Memorial Day and Christmas or Hanukkah.

You can make some simple or elaborate floral arrangements which you then take to a person's grave.

Keep a list of clients and provide a recurring service, both annually and to remember recurring holidays.

76. Dry & Sell Dried Flowers.

Dried flowers last much longer than live cut flowers and are much easier to produce, maintain and sell.

Learning to dry flowers is quite simple. You can learn how to dry flowers using glycerin, an oven or freeze drying.

There are two main ways to make money with dried flowers. The one is to dry flower arrangements for others. The other is to raise or buy flowers and then dry them.

You can offer a service to dry flowers from weddings, anniversaries, and other special occasions. Some will want them for decorating, others will want them for scrapbooks or shadow boxes.

You can sell dried flowers to crafts stores or hobbyists.

Some people use them for centerpieces and decorating. Some use dried flowers on sandals and clothing.

You can raise your own flowers, harvest wild ones, or buy flowers to dry.

77. Make & Sell Artificial Flower Arrangements.

Some artificial flowers make very nice arrangements. They are easy to work with and last a very long time.

I bought nice artificial flowers in our local *Dollar Tree* and made some very attractive artificial arrangements which were greatly appreciated. I made one for the widow of a local florist. I attached a note which said, *Just as your love for your husband will not fade, neither will these flowers*. She told me she placed it on the mantle next to her husband's urn.

These can make nice memorials for gravesites, but you must make sure the cemetery allows them.

78. Make & Sell Door Wreaths.

For many years people decorated their doors with wreaths at Christmas Time. There are some who decorate their doors year-round with decorative seasonal wreaths.

The traditional Christmas wreaths were made from pine boughs, ribbons, and bells. Now many of them are made from artificial materials.

Grape vines are often used to make wreaths. Some other vines work well. Though they are quite hearty, I advise against using poison ivy vines.

If you plan to buy artificial wreaths to decorate, you can maximize your profit buying them after a holiday season.

To make seasonal wreaths you just add different seasonal looking items. Hearts and red accents look good for Valentine's Day. Shamrocks and green accents work well for St. Patrick's Day. Red, White, and Blue accents work great for patriotic holidays.

Make Money with Food

If you like making food items, and other people like what you make, this section might contain the right income generating match for you.

There are many ways to make money with food. Some methods can be easy while some are a bit more complicated than others.

It is likely you will need a license or approval from a health department to sell food items in your municipality.

79. Bake & Sell Cookies.

Many people like cookies. You may be able to generate some significant income baking and selling cookies.

One day I was invited to a local Senior Center to hear a man tell the story of how he made a million dollars selling cookies. I was intrigued so I went to hear him.

That man told how he tried to start a variety of business and how none of them worked. He said when he was discouraged he would go home and make himself a batch of chocolate chip cookies as comfort food. His friends liked his cookies and encouraged him to sell them. He finally decided to sell his cookies and was very successful.

His cookie business grew to the point where his cookies were sold in stores across America. One day he sold his business to another company for more than a million dollars. His name was *Wally Amos*. His cookies were called *Famous Amos Chocolate Chip Cookies*.

The night I heard him speak, he asked if we would like the recipe for his famous cookies. We were all delighted at that offer. He then held up a bag of *Nestles Semi-Sweet Chocolate Chips*, and showed us the back of the bag. On the back of the bag is a recipe for Chocolate Chip Cookies. He said that is the recipe he used. We were amazed.

Perhaps you can be the next Wally Amos? Start small and see what happens.

To make money selling cookies you need a good recipe and places to sell them. You may be able to sell them at farmers markets but will probably do better marketing them to events and to local eateries.

Many people like it when you make products with all-natural ingredients. You can do that simply or very extensively with a local farm-to-table emphasis.

The recipe is the easy part. Consider starting with some basic flavors people like, such as chocolate chip cookies and sugar cookies. You can use commercial mixes and customize them or craft your own.

It is always good to develop your own signature varieties. A big part of that could be the way you shape and decorate your cookies. Well-decorated cookies sell best.

Many people are gluten intolerant and cannot eat

traditional cookies. I am one of those people. Most of the gluten-free cookies I have tasted are awful. If you could develop some good tasting gluten-free cookies you can increase your profitability.

You need to determine where to sell these. You could sell to restaurants, coffeehouses, cafeterias, local theatres, or delicatessens. You should also target special events.

For local eateries you may want to have an agreement where you provide one or two signature cookies one or two days a week.

You may want to offer a once or twice-a-week cookie delivery service to some offices or other businesses.

You need to price your cookies competitively. Look around and see what bakeries and other businesses are charging in your area.

Like any other items you sell, you need a way for people to know you have items available. You probably should have a basic website and use social media. Develop a logo. Make some business cards and fliers.

Send out news releases with pictures when you provide cookies for events or when you develop a new recipe.

80. Bake & Sell Cupcakes.

Selling cupcakes can be very profitable, maybe even more profitable than selling cookies. You can sell them in small quantities or for bigger venues. Cupcakes have become very popular at weddings, anniversaries, office parties, concerts, events, and other functions. They are much easier to serve than cakes.

In most cases cupcakes cost less than wedding cakes. The average wedding has between 150-200 guests. Of course, some have more people, and some have less. The average wedding cake cost $7.50 to $12 per slice. That means a wedding cake for 150 guests will cost between $1,125 to $1,800. Cupcakes for weddings cost between $2.50 to $3.50 each. That means cupcakes for 150 guests will cost between $375 to $525. That lower cost will appeal to some. Those are average prices. Some can cost more.

The same principles for selling cookies apply to selling cupcakes.

Do not forget to make gluten-free cupcakes. There are many gluten intolerant people who feel left out at a weddings or other events when cake and cupcakes are served which they cannot eat. If you provide gluten-free varieties you will probably generate additional business.

You need a good recipe for the cupcakes and the frosting. It is also very important that you decorate and display them well.

You need to determine where to sell them. Most people with a cupcake business try to sell to weddings and other events. You may want to do that, but you could also bake some which you sell to restaurants, coffeehouses, cafeterias, local theatres, or delicatessens.

For local eateries you may want an agreement where you provide one or two types of signature cupcakes one or two days a week.

You may want to offer a delivery service to some offices of other businesses once or twice a week. That alone could be a very profitable focus for your business.

Market yourself using social media and new releases.

81. Make & Sell Fudge.

Fudge is a decadent treat many people enjoy. There are so many varieties and recipes available. If you have a good recipe it is very likely you can generate additional income making and selling fudge.

Many of the same principles for baking and selling cookies and cupcakes also apply to selling fudge.

I have seen fudge for sale at many tourist attractions. Those places usually do not make their own fudge, they buy the fudge and resell it. There may be some tourist attractions, hotels, or gift shops near you where you could sell your fudge.

I have often seen fudge for sale at events and at Flea Markets. Some of the best fudge I ever bought was at the annual *Warrensburg Garage Sale* in Warrensburg, New York in the Adirondack Mountains.

You could piggyback a fudge selling endeavor with selling cookies or cupcakes and could possibly sell them to the same places. Your fudge might become part of a nice dessert menu at some local eateries.

82. Do Lunch Deliveries.

You may be able to generate extra income doing lunch time deliveries for a local restaurant or delicatessen or you could make your own food and deliver that.

This could work especially well if you offer specialty menus. There are many possibilities. You could be a direct *farm-to-market* lunch source, specializing in local items. You could offer gluten-free, vegetarian, vegan, low-sodium, heart-healthy or totally organic lunch menus.

Other options could be to offer ethnic foods or specialize in chili or soup. Or you could offer some good old-fashioned sandwiches or home cooking.

You could offer this service one or more days a week. If you live in a larger area you may want to provide your service in a different area on a different day of the week.

83. Provide a Coffee Service & Snacks.

Years ago, it was not unusual for people providing a coffee service and snacks to drive a food truck to offices, garages, factories, and other businesses on a regular basis.

I worked at one place where one of the highlights of the day for the employees was to go to the coffee service truck and see what pastries and goodies were offered that day.

You may be able to provide a simple service like this to some businesses in your area. You could possible partner with a local coffee shop and make deliveries for them and add some additional items you make yourself.

84. Have a Food Cart or Truck.

This is similar to the coffee service method except here you have a food truck or food cart which you drive to one or more locations. You can also do this and earn extra income selling some specialty food items at fairs, carnivals, flea markets, festivals, and other events.

In some areas, food carts/trucks sell a wide variety of foods. Some sell ethnic specialties, some sell seafood, fried foods, or fried dough. There are many possibilities.

Many of the popular food carts in our area sell hot dogs. They call them dirty water dogs. I find it hard to understand why so many people love to them.

One day I saw a man leaving a famous fast food restaurant in our area. He was carrying a tray of rolls. I asked if he just bought some day-old rolls from the restaurant. He told me no. He said the restaurant ordered extra rolls for him for his hot dog stand. I asked him if he made much money selling hot dogs at his stand by the side of the road. He told me he earned more money doing that than he did when he was a white-collar office worker.

This method is usually regulated by the local department of health. In our area, you cannot operate a food cart unless you are a veteran of the armed forces.

85. Cook for Others.

Earning extra income by cooking for others is a very old time-tested way to generate income. Years ago, many people did this by cooking extra food for their families and then taking some of that food to someone else.

There is a need for people to cook for others. Some people do not like to cook, and some are not able to cook and will gladly pay others to cook for them.

You may be able to earn extra income by making yourself available to cook for others. You could prepare meals for one or more people or for families. You could cook one or more meals a day, one or more days a week.

I know many single guys who do not cook at all and could be interested in a service like this, especially if the food looks and tastes good. That is one of the keys to being successful at this. The food you prepare must look good and taste good.

There is also a growing market of senior citizens who need others to cook for them. There are also people who need meals while they are recuperating at home from surgery. Families are always looking for people who can provide meals for their loved ones.

When you cook for specific people you will learn what they like and how much you need to make.

If you use this method, you should develop a weekly or monthly menu of the meals you can make. You can always expand on that.

86.   Make Dressings & Dips.

I have seen numerous people sell dressings and dips at Flea Markets. Those sellers come back year after year, so they must be generating income with this method.

Some people have themes, such as Southwestern, Cajun, Maple, Honey, Gluten-Free and Organic.

Some sell ready to use dressings and dips, others sell special packets of ingredients for you to make it yourself.

87.   Sell Turtles.

Trapping and selling turtles is an international business. Many of the turtles caught and sold are used to make turtle soup. Many people consider turtle soup a delicacy. In order to make turtle soup, you need a turtle. I do not recommend selling the family pet turtle for this.

A turtle can provide you with a low cost, low calorie, low fat, and low cholesterol meal. It could also be a source of extra income.

Many different types of turtles can be used for making turtle soup but one of the more popular ones is the

Snapping Turtle. That is because they grow larger than most other turtles, so they have much more meat per turtle. The average *Box Turtle* only weighs about 1-2 pounds. The average *snapping turtle* weighs between 10-35 pounds. Many get much larger. One *Snapping Turtle* was caught which weighed 600 pounds.

It is important to remember *Snapping Turtles* have very powerful jaws. Those jaws can inflict some serious wounds. Many *Snapping Turtles* can easily snap off one of your fingers. Be warned, although *Snapping Turtles* may appear to be slow, they can move their heads very fast and bite you and inflict serious harm.

I had a neighbor who frequently went to New York City to sell items at a Flea Market. On his drive to the city, he purposefully took a route which took him by reservoirs where he often saw *Snapping Turtles* walking near the side of the road. He would catch *Snapping Turtles* before they met an unfortunate end and became *road smear*. When he got to the city, he said he sold them to some restaurants for turtle soup. At that time, he received about $100 for a 30-pound turtle. He said that provided a few benefits: the turtle ended their life with more meaning than being traumatically obliterated by a truck or car; someone enjoyed some turtle soup; and my neighbor and his family reaped a financial benefit.

It is very important to check to see if there are turtle catching and selling regulations in your area. Be very careful if you see turtles wearing ninja costumes.

88. Sell Fish.

Selling fish has been a way many people generated income for thousands of years.

For hundreds of years my mother's family in Norway made their living as fishermen. There is a very big world-wide market for fish.

You can either catch fish and sell them or, if you live near some docks or a fish market, you can buy fish and resell them. Some people catch fish and sell them by the side of the road. Some sell them to markets or restaurants.

I had a friend who lived in Endicott, New York who made money catching fish caught in pools of water next to the Susquehanna River each season when it flooded. He would take his wagon and go along the river and harvest large carp. He then took them back to town and sold them for a handsome profit.

It is very important you check with local regulations if you intend to catch and sell fish. Many areas have specific dates when you are allowed to catch fish. They usually state the minimum size for keeping a fish and a daily limit on how many you may catch and keep.

89. Sell Vegetables.

Many people like to eat fresh vegetables. Many people do not realize the people who sell vegetables are rarely the people who grow them. Vegetables are a big resell market.

You can raise vegetables (next method) or buy vegetables from farmers or vegetable markets to resell.

There is a big vegetable market at the north end of Manhattan, in Spanish Harlem near the Fordham Avenue Bridge. Many people go there early in the morning to buy vegetables to resell.

You may be able to put together a simple farm stand, which you operate one or more days a week, where you sell vegetables. You may also be able to resell vegetables at a local farmers market.

You can also buy and resell vegetables to restaurants or grocery stores or direct to people. You can advertise yourself as a *farm-to-table service*.

90. Harvest Fruits & Vegetables to Resell.

You may want to consider going to a farm or orchard to harvest fruits and vegetables to resell. I am not talking about getting just one basket of apples. I am talking about doing some serious harvesting. You can harvest both to help feed your family and to sell some.

The concept of getting food direct from the farm to the table appeals to many people. One reason is because the food you harvest fresh often has more flavor than what people buy in a store.

This is also a good form of exercise and can be a productive family or dating activity.

There are many types of farms where you can harvest vegetables or fruit. In our area, the popular ones grow and sell strawberries, blueberries, and apples. In other areas it might be peaches, pecans, or potatoes.

You can make money by going to a pick-your-own farm and then re-selling some, or all, of what you pick.

There are some places where they will pay you to harvest. When I was in college I earned money working as an apple picker.

91. Raise a Garden & Sell Vegetables.

One of the most profitable ways to make money with vegetables can be to raise them yourself. That has two benefits: it provides food for your family, which is basically generating income; and second, it can provide crops to sell, which can generate additional income.

Many people like organic vegetables. Organic vegetables are those raised without fertilizer or pesticides If you can raise vegetables organically, you can make more money. We had some friends who raise vegetables organically and then sold them to a research hospital. They received a significantly higher price for their vegetables, and they helped people at the same time.

If you have a lawn why waste money mowing it? Unless you use your lawn for recreation, why not convert it into a garden and make it work for you.

Benefits of Making Your Lawn a Garden:

☐ You will not have the expense of mowing it.

- ☐ You can help reduce your grocery bill.
- ☐ You may be able to raise enough food to sell.

If you want the most productive garden possible, I highly recommend, *The Joy of Gardening*, by Dick Raymond. It is one of the most practical books I ever read. Get a used copy on *Amazon.com*.

People from other countries are amazed how much land we waste in America. Instead of using our land for growing productive crops, we have big lawns covered with grass, just to look at. We spend money to keep mowing the grass, so we can look at a mowed lawn.

Why not make your land productive and convert some, or all of your yard into a vegetable garden?

If you do not have a lawn, you can get some type of containers and plant some vegetables. You can also use old buckets or even some big old pots and pans.

Someone posted pictures on *Facebook* showing how they took old roof gutters, converted them into strawberry planters and grew many strawberries on their deck.

For many years, I planted vegetable gardens in places with harsh environments and short growing seasons. In upstate New Hampshire *(which seemed close to the North Pole)*, we could not plant until Father's Day, which is in the middle of June. We had our first frost start at the end of August. Yet we had productive gardens.

We grew gardens in both small areas and in a very large area. Some vegetables, like corn, do not work well unless you have a large garden area and a lot of direct sunlight.

Some people start vegetables inside in containers and then take them outside when the risk of frost is gone. They bring them back inside when it gets frosty. That extends their growing season and increases their productivity.

The following are some simple easy to grow vegetables. These will grow in many different places. You can also grow all of these in a 5-gallon bucket. Place them on a porch, deck, or inside near a window with a lot of sunlight.

Lettuce

Plant *leaf lettuce*. It is easier to grow and more productive than *head lettuce*. When it is at least five to six inches high, give it a crew cut and you will have delicious fresh lettuce to sell. It will regrow, and you can continue to harvest fresh lettuce as needed.

You may want to combine this lettuce with other vegetables and sell them as salads.

Radishes

Radishes grow very fast and are nutritious. People like to eat them raw, in salads or pickled They make good *kimchi*. Unlike many other vegetables, radishes store well, extending the season to sell them.

Green Beans

Green Beans are easy to grow and quite productive. I recommend you grow *Bush Beans (just remember some Democrats do not like Bush Beans).*

As long as you keep picking green beans, before they develop big seeds, they will keep producing. You can let them go to seed and use those seeds as dried beans or save them to plant next year.

Beans are called a *green manure,* not because they taste like manure (*though I do not know what manure tastes like)* but like manure, if you turn the plants back into the soil, they replenish the soil with vital nutrients.

Peppers

There are many varieties of peppers, from sweet to dangerously hot. They love lots of sunlight. They store well in a freezer for a long time.

If you have limited space, peppers can grow in a 5-gallon bucket. You can then extend their growing season by taking them inside when it starts to frost and place them in a sunny spot.

Cucumbers

There are a number of varieties of cucumbers. Some

varieties produce cucumbers 6-8 inches long. Some grow to be more than 14 inches long.

You can grow cucumbers in a container but will not find them easy to bring back indoors. You can place a trellis or lattice in a container for the cucumbers.

If you harvest cucumbers before their seeds get too big, the plants will keep producing more.

Cucumbers are very good for pickling and will last a long time that way.

Squash

There are many varieties of squash, such as zucchini, butternut, acorn, summer, and winter squash.

Squash is a vine. It is related to the cucumber. If you grow them next to each other, they cross-pollinate. What they produce that year will be fine, but do not plant the seeds for the next year.

You can grow squash in a container, but their vines spread out much more than cucumbers. They need a lot of room.

Tomatoes

You can grow tomatoes almost any place. They can do well in 5-gallon buckets.

Some Different Varieties of Tomatoes.

- **Big Boy** or **Beefsteak** - These are the more traditional large tomatoes, which take a long time to grow. They are quite juicy and are very good for sandwiches, salads, or beverages.
- **Roma** – These are smaller oblong shaped tomatoes. These are a meatier tomato with less juice. You can use Roma's in salads, but they work especially well in sauces because they are more meaty than juicy.
- **Cherry** or **Grape** - These are small tomatoes, which grow very fast and abundant. We harvest more than 50 a week from as few as four

plants. They are great in salads. They are juicy which is good for making beverages and soups.

☐ **Orange** or **Yellow** - These have less acid, which give them a wonderful taste for sandwiches or salads.

Did you hear about the three tomatoes who went for a walk? One of the tomatoes kept lagging behind. That annoyed the other tomatoes. Finally, the biggest tomato went back and stomped on the tomato, who kept lagging behind, and said, *Ketchup!*

92. Raise & Sell Corn.

Raising and selling corn can generate additional income but it takes a lot of work.

I know two brothers who bought some farm land with money from their paper route. They planted corn, which they sold. They earned enough money this way to pay for both of them to attend college.

There is a lot of good land no longer in production. Many farmers are growing older and have cut back on their corn production. Keeping fields in production can help keep a person's property taxes lower. You may be able to work out something where you can raise corn by either renting some fields or doing some profit sharing.

Learn the different types of corn. *Sweet corn* is raised for human consumption. *Field corn* is raised to be feed for livestock in America but is consumed by people in other countries. Some corn is raised for corn syrup, corn starch, corn powder or for the commercial market.

You may be able to work for someone else raising and selling corn or you may be able to do this by yourself or with some family or friends.

93. Sell Seeds.

Many people buy seeds. You may be able to generate extra income selling seeds. You will probably earn more income if you raise your own seeds and sell them.

Most people go to a market to buy their seeds. Some people buy them through catalogs, online, or at farmers markets.

Many commercial seeds are treated so they will not rot and so they will germinate and grow. Many people buy those because it is convenient. There is a growing segment of the population who want seeds which are not treated.

You can grow crops which are not treated with chemicals and let some go to seed, or you can buy some organically grown crops which have gone to seed, in order to harvest seeds to resell.

Some people will gladly let you harvest crops which have over ripened and gone to seed. You can save the seeds from those crops and sell them.

Some seeds sell for a significant amount of money, especially if they come from prize winning crops.

Every year there are contests to see who can grow the biggest pumpkin. You may want to try that. One prize was more than $15,000. Though there is usually prize money for the winner, one of the greatest sources of income is selling the seeds from the winning pumpkins.

The number of seeds in a pumpkin vary according to its size. One standard is to estimate 10 to 16 seeds per rib (the segments, around the pumpkin, running from the top to the bottom). If a pumpkin has 20 ribs it would yield between 200 and 320 seeds. Larger pumpkins have larger seeds and sometimes have more seeds than small ones.

Individual seeds from prize winning pumpkins sell for as low as $3 per seed to as high as $58 per seed, depending on the size of the pumpkin. If your pumpkin had 200 seeds and sold for $3 each, you would have $600. If they sold for $50 each you would have $1,000.

94. Raise & Sell Berries.

You may be able to generate some good seasonal income from berries if you have land and patience to do it.

My sister-in-law's father planted a raspberry patch in his backyard and sold them to local farmer's markets. Raspberries only produce ripe fruit for a few weeks, yet he told me he made enough money from his small berry patch to pay his school and property taxes every year.

Some berries grow on vines like grapes. Some grow in brambles with thorns, like blackberries and raspberries. Some grow on bushes, like blueberries and highbush cranberries. Strawberries grow along the ground.

The space needed for planting berries varies by the type of plant. If you plant a few varieties of berries you need to keep them at least 300 feet from the other varieties or you will have cross-pollination.

Most berries tend to be fragile, have a very short harvest season and must be marketed quickly. You have a narrow window to sell them.

Grapes tend to be heartier and have a longer season than other berries. They usually grow well in the same climate as apples so some people plant rows of dwarf apple trees and rows of grape vines nearby.

The market for berries is usually farmers markets, fruit stands, local grocery stores and some restaurants.

95. Make & Sell Jam or Jelly.

Making and selling jams and jelly is a very good way to extend the profitability of berries or fruits.

Many people love good jams and jellies. You may want to generate some income making and selling your own. You can make these using your own fruits or ones you harvested or purchased.

If you put your finished product into canning jars it will look nice and probably sell better.

96. Sell Maple Syrup.

You may be able to generate income buying and reselling maple syrup or doing your own syrup operation.

It takes a lot of work to make maple syrup, but it can generate income in a short amount of time in late winter and sometimes in early spring.

If you like maple syrup, and have enough trees in your area, if you collect a large quantity of sap and boil it down you will have some delicious maple syrup.

In our area, maple syrup is quite expensive. A gallon of maple syrup costs more than 15 gallons of gasoline. It sells for even more when it is sold in smaller quantities such as quarts and pints. Those are the sizes most people want.

We made 20-40 gallons of delicious maple syrup each year for a few years. At around $50 per gallon, 40 gallons would sell for $2,000.

Maple season starts when the temperature is above freezing during the day and below freezing at night. Those conditions make the sap run. Once the nighttime temperatures stay above freezing the sap will change and smell different and not produce good syrup.

There are different methods you can use to make maple syrup. We used a very inexpensive method. Our only expense was to buy metal taps for the trees, a large plastic garbage container, and containers for the finished syrup.

We hand drilled one to four holes for taps at a slight upward angle in each tree, using an old-fashioned hand drill. You could use a cordless drill to do this step.

We then cut a hole in the side of plastic gallon milk containers, near the handles, and placed them over the taps to collect the sap. We left the lid on those containers.

When the milk jugs were full we transferred the sap from them into a large plastic garbage can. We then brought that back to the house and boiled down the sap.

It usually takes about 40 ounces of sap and a lot of boiling to make one ounce of maple syrup. To make a gallon of syrup you boil down about 40 gallons of sap. That means you will expel some 39 gallons of liquid into the air. If you do that inside on your stove, you will be burning a lot of expensive fuel. You will also end up with sticky moisture in your house. We learned that the hard way and moved our maple syrup operation outside.

Our trees had a much higher sugar content and it only took 32 gallons of sap to produce one gallon of syrup.

The first time we did this, we used some old bricks and made an outside fireplace. We placed an old refrigerator shelf on top of that. We then placed six old cake pans on top of the shelf and put sap in the pans and rotated the sap in a counterclockwise direction as it boiled down.

If you intend to make maple syrup for a number or years, you could get a nice stainless-steel evaporator and make the process a lot easier.

We used a lot of scrap wood and old fallen down trees and branches to make the fire at no cost. It takes a lot of time and patience to make maple syrup that way. We looked at it as a productive no-cost family activity.

As the sap boils down, you need to move that sap from one pan to another. We choose a counterclockwise direction. We rotated the boiled down sap, pan by pan, then replenished the sap in the first pan. That way the last pan had the highest sugar concentration. With most of the water removed from that last pan we brought that inside and did the final boiling inside with no sticky mess. The result was delicious expensive maple syrup.

Later, we used an old wood stove on our porch. We still used the same method with the six cake pans. It worked a lot better on the wood stove.

You can place the finished maple syrup into professional containers or you can put it in mason jars. Pint or quart containers are the best size.

Some people just collect the maple sap and sell it to local maple syrup producers. You may want to simplify and do that to earn some income.

If you make syrup you can sell it at a farm stand or just put out a sign by the side of the road and sell the syrup from your home. That is the most profitable method.

Some people sell maple syrup to other farm stands or

at Farmer's Markets. You may also be able to sell it to local grocery stores, gift shops and restaurants.

97. Plant Fruit or Nut Trees.

It takes about three years for fruit or nut trees to produce income, but then they can provide income for many years. You can sell the fruit or nuts or make products with them.

You need a yard and must live in an area where you can grow apples, oranges, peaches, cherries, pecans or some other kind of fruit or nuts.

Most people think you need a lot of land to make money this way, that is not true. You can make some income even with only a handful of trees. The bigger your lawn, the more trees you can plant. You may want to convert your whole yard into an orchard.

Ideally you should plant fruit trees about 10 feet apart. If you have a yard which is 100 feet x 50 feet, you could grow 5 rows of 10 trees for a total of 50 trees.

Many people use dwarf trees because they are easier to maintain and harvest. They also select varieties which ripen at different times. That provides a longer harvest, which allows you to sell fruit over a longer period of time.

Some backyard growers plant trees as close as 4 feet apart. If you planted trees 4 feet apart in rows 8 feet apart, that would make it easier to mow. If you do that use dwarf trees and select varieties which ripen at different times.

It takes about three years for a fruit tree to produce fruit. In the first and second year, in the spring, you need to cut back the new growth to half its height and need to do it again in the summer. It is a good idea to remove any fruit which grows during the first two years, so the growth goes back into the trees.

In the third year, you determine the maximum height you will allow the trees to grow. You need to keep them pruned to that height every summer. That year they should start to produce fruit.

To get larger fruit you need to thin out the fruit while it is small. The remaining ones will grow larger.

If you want a profitable crop, protect your trees from wild creatures who love to eat them probably more than you. That includes: birds, deer, racoon, and squirrels. The best protection is barriers such as fences and netting.

The following are some average yields per tree for dwarf trees: Apples, 1-4 bushels; Apricots , 1-3 bushels; Cherries, 15-20 quarts; Nectarine, 2-3 bushels; Peaches, 1-3 bushels; Pears, 2-3 bushels; and Plums, ½-2 bushels.

Nut trees take much more space and some, such a Pecan Trees, take about 10 years to produce a good crop.

98. Make & Sell Pies or Cheesecake.

Many people love pies and cheesecake, including me. Some people would rather have a pie than most cakes.

Some people make *good* pies and others make *great* pies. If you can learn to make some *great* pies you could probably generate a steady source of income. This is also another good way to extend the profitability of raising berries, fruit, and nuts.

I was disappointed when I was diagnosed with gluten intolerance. That means I should not eat grains such as wheat, which is usually the main ingredient in pie crusts and cakes. I am waiting for someone to figure out how to make a good tasting gluten-free pie crust.

One way to market your pies is make a few pies each week for some restaurants, coffee shops or eateries. You may offer a few standard pies or a weekly surprise special.

Perhaps you could provide a weekly pie or cheesecake delivery service to individuals.

99. Raise Your Own Chickens.

You may be able to make money raising chickens for meat or eggs. It takes a big commitment. Make sure you understand what is involved and are willing to take on a task like this. If you follow this route, do not *chicken out*.

The cost for raising meat and eggs is similar to what some grocery stores charge for their standard genetically engineered chickens, which they feed with artificially medicated food. The meat and eggs you raise will be organically grown and can be sold for a higher price.

If you plan to raise chickens or any other livestock to sell for meat, no matter how cute they are, it is a good idea not to give them names.

Before attempting to raise chickens or any livestock, check with your local zoning department to see if they allow you to raise what you desire.

Chickens for Meat or to Lay Eggs?

☐ Chickens to Eat

Cornish X is the standard meat chicken sold in grocery stores. They grow fast and are the most common and productive ones to raise for meat.

☐ Chickens to Lay Eggs

If you raise the *Cornish X* for meat and plan to raise others for eggs, get different colored hens to lay eggs so you do not eat the wrong ones. *Cornish X* are white.

Some of the non-white breeds, which produce the most eggs are the *Ameraucana/Easter Egg Chicken* (300 eggs per year), *California Gray* (300 eggs per year) or *Rhode Island Red* (250 eggs per year).

Costs for Raising Chickens:

☐ Chicken House/Coop

You need about 4 sq. feet per chicken in a coop and 8-10 sq. feet pen area per chicken. You also need a light for inside the coop. An average coop for 10 chickens will cost $400 and up.

☐ Buy Chicks

The average cost to buy a good chick is $5. If you buy ones to lay and ones to eat, you can keep them together but as already stated, make sure you get different colored ones, so you do not sell the wrong ones.

You can often get chicks after Easter, at a reduced price or for free, from people who gave chicks as pets. I know some people who get them for free from schools, which raise chicks for a couple of months as a class project.

☐ Feed

Each chick eats 10-12 pounds of feed before they are fully-grown. Feed cost about $15-30 for 50 pounds. It cost about $10 in feed to get one chick to laying size. After that time, it costs about $0.90 a week. Ten chickens eat about 50 pounds of food a month. The feed for chickens raised for meat cost more than for laying chickens. If you keep both together, you can use a general feed for both but will either get less eggs or less meaty chickens.

☐ Bedding

Use straw, not hay. You need to change the bedding to keep down odors. They smell bad fast.

When Can You Eat a Chicken?

It may surprise some people, but a *Cornish X* chicken will be ready to eat when it is about 8 weeks old. They will dress out to 5-6 pounds. It cost about $1.20 per pound to raise one to that point. That cost is between 50-75% less than buying an organically grown chicken in the store.

How Many Eggs a Week?

The average hen starts to lay eggs at about 6 months old and lays an average of 3-5 eggs per week for two years, and sometimes up to 5 years.

The number of eggs tends to drop during the time of year with less daylight and increases with more daylight.

Ten laying hens can produce about 30-50 eggs a week. Feed costs about $11 a week. With bedding, it cost about $3 per dozen eggs if the hens produce 40 eggs a week. That is on par with what many stores charge for regular eggs.

If you raise yours organically, in some areas you can sell organic eggs for $4-7 per dozen.

100. Raise Rabbits.

You can raise and sell rabbits as pets or for food. They have nice soft pelts, which you can use to make clothing.

I stayed with a family in Quebec who started raising rabbits to provide food for their family. Eventually they had more rabbits than they needed. They sold some for meat. It turned into a family business and helped support the family and paid for college for all their children.

Rabbits are considered the easiest animal to raise for food. Some people consider them a delicacy. They are a low-fat, low-cholesterol meat.

Some scientists call rabbits, *the food of the future* because they have the lowest environmental impact, require the least amount of space and are so productive. You can raise two does and one buck and offspring, in a hutch about 3 feet by 10 feet.

Rabbits multiply quickly, faster than many math students. Two does and one buck produce an average of 40-50 offspring a year. The offspring yield three plus pounds of meat each, so you can get 120-150 pounds of meat a year.

Most people breed each doe about once every three months. Many people stagger the breeding between two does. The young are born in about 30 days. They nurse for five to six weeks. After that, place them in a separate hutch.

Most people eat rabbits when they are 8-12 weeks old. After 12 weeks, the cost of feeding them can pass the cost you save by selling them or eating them. The best time to start to sell them is when they are 8 weeks old.

For healthy stock, it is recommended to replace does every two to three years and bucks every three to four years.

There are many breeds of rabbits. If you are raising them sell as food you want the meatier ones.

The *Chinchilla* is a very popular medium-sized meat rabbit. They weigh about 8-10 pounds when they are ready to eat and yield about 3 pounds of meat.

The *Californian* is another good rabbit for meat.

Some breeds have more desirable pelts. The *New Zealand White* is a medium-sized meat rabbit. It has a white pelt, which sells for more than others.

It is important to feed the rabbits a good hay or pellets from a suspended manger or they will contaminate their food with their waste.

Various growers estimate the cost of raising rabbits to average $1-2 per pound of meat produced. That is much lower than the cost of most meat in the grocery store. In some areas, organically grown rabbit meat sells for $6 per pound. If you feed them standard pellets, they are no longer considered organic and will sell for less per pound.

To maximize your return be sure to sell their pelts or have them treated and make things to sell.

101. Raise Pigs/Hogs.

Raising pigs for meat can be very productive. Pork, the meat from pigs, is eaten by a larger percentage of the world's population (40%). That is more than beef (32%), poultry (22%) or sheep (6%).

Pigs are favorites for food because they put on more weight in proportion to the amount of feed they consume and require less supervision than any other livestock.

Many people use the terms *pig* and *hog* interchangeably. Technically, they are *swine*. They are called *pigs* until they reach about 120 pounds, then they are called *hogs*.

It takes a serious commitment to raise pigs, but they provide a lot of meat to sell.

You need a place with a lot of room to house them. They

do not do well in a house or in an apartment in the city. They are hard to hide from fellow tenants. The best place for them is a stall in a barn, or in a large pen with shelter. My wife's family kept their pigs in a stall in the barn.

Pigs also need food, water, bedding, and a way to transport them to a butcher.

A few summer camps and conference centers I spoke at give table scraps from their dining rooms to local pig farmers. You may be able to make such an arrangement to get some extra food and save money feeding your pigs.

Some dairy farmers, who raise pigs, feed their pigs a lot of milk. People consider a milk-fed pig one of the tastiest.

Pigs are social animals, so it is always a good idea to raise at least two together or to live in the pen with them.

The *University of Kentucky, School of Agriculture*, claims pigs yield as high as 70-73% meat products for carcass weight.

It is usually more profitable to get young pigs in the spring, raise them during the summer when food is more abundant, and butcher them in the fall when they weigh about 170 pounds. That will give you 102-128 pounds of boneless trimmed meat. It cost about $375 to raise a pig during that time. That includes housing, feed, bedding, and processing. If you get 110 pounds of meat you would break even at $3.40 per pound.

The 2018 average retail price for boneless pork is between $8 to $12 per pound, depending on the cut. If you sold 110 pounds of pork for an average price of $10 per pound, you would receive $1,100. If you subtract the $375 cost of raising the pig, you would profit $725 per pig. Most people raise at least 2 pigs at a time. If you do the slaughtering and processing yourself, your cost drops to $215 and your profit raises to $885 or more per pig or $1,770 or more for 2 pigs.

102. Raise Cattle to Sell Meat & Milk.

Raising a cow to provide milk or meat has been a life-sustaining stable for many people for thousands of years. If you raise a few cattle, you may be able to generate some significant income selling meat or milk.

If you live in the country, as my wife did, it is easier to raise a cow than in the city. In the city you need a big enclosed courtyard or penthouse and must hide your cow.

Many people raise cattle for milk and meat. You can use their milk to make butter, cheese, and cottage cheese.

Some breeds are better for milk, such as *Holstein* or *Jersey*. *Herford* or *Angus* are better for meat.

You can generate extra income by using the hide from any cow to make leather for clothing.

A *Jersey* cow usually produces the most milk with the highest butter fat content. One *Jersey* cow will produce about 5-6 gallons of milk a day with 5% butterfat.

As soon as a cow has a calf, no matter what her breed, you can milk her. You can keep milking a cow for a few years, as long as you milk her at least once a day or have her with nursing calves. You do not need to milk them twice a day. Beef cows can be milked but do not produce as much milk as dairy cows.

Here is a very important warning from a city kid, do not try milking male cows.

Cows eat a lot of food. You can reduce feeding costs if you have a grazing area. You need about 1-2 acres per cow. Instead of grazing their cows some people keep their cows in a small barnyard and barn and bring all of the food to the cows. Some dairy farmers prefer that method, so they can monitor and control what their cows eat.

Whatever a cow eats affects the taste of her milk. That is one reason milk from California often tastes different than milk from New York.

Cows eat about 30-40 pounds of hay per day. That is about one small 40-pound bale of hay a day. In our area, those small bales sell for $5-10 each. That means just the hay alone will cost you $5-10 per day, per cow, if you do not graze your cows.

It takes about 10 minutes to feed a cow and 20 minutes to milk one. You only need to milk them once a day if you allow their calves to stay with them during the day. Most people milk their cows twice a day to increase the amount of milk they produce. Many commercial operations milk their cows three times a day.

It also takes about 5-10 minutes a day to provide water manually and 15 minutes per day to clean up manure.

You can eat any cow, but some are better to raise for beef. Older cattle are tougher. I know some dairy farmers who butcher older milk cows, which no longer produce milk. They mainly make them into hamburger meat. Old dairy cows are the main source of meat for some of the major fast food restaurants.

Many who raise cattle for meat, get heifers in the spring, raise them for 24-30 months, then butcher them.

Some cattle raised for meat are strictly grass fed, some are grain feed.

The *University of Illinois* determined the cost to raise a beef cow can range from $190-400 per year. They claim It is possible some people can do it for $200 per year.

If you buy a calf for $900 and spend $600 to take care of it for three years, you will have a total cost of $1,500. At the end of three years, an *Angus* steer weighs an average of 1,200 pounds and produces 530 pounds of meat. That places the cost per pound at $2.83 per pound. In our area, we are happy if we find ground beef on sale at $2.99 per pound. Many cuts of beef sell for more than $10 per pound. If you sell the beef for an average $8 per pound and you get 530 pounds of meat that would be $4,240, minus $1,500 cost to raise one, yielding a net profit of $2,740 each. If you raise 10 that would produce $27,740 profit.

According to the *University of Kentucky, School of Agriculture*, grain feed cattle yield about 60-63% meat for their carcass weight. They claim grass fed cattle yield about 56-58%. Their study shows a 1,200-pound dairy cow will produce much less, coming in at 386 pounds of meat.

103. Raise Sheep for Food & Wool.

Sheep are one of the least expensive livestock to raise, and have one of the biggest returns.

Sheep are social animals, so it is a good idea to raise at least two.

Unlike chicken or pigs, sheep can provide milk and wool. You can use the wool to make clothing.

There is another benefit of raising sheep. If you have a hard time sleeping you can count your sheep to help you fall asleep.

You need a field if you plan to raise sheep. Sheep love to graze, which can greatly reduce feeding expenses. It takes about one acre per 6 sheep.

Sheep are good for keeping fields from growing up. They eat many plants, which cattle or horses will not eat. Sheep can stay outside year-round in many areas, if you provide them with three-sided, roofed shelters.

If your sheep get out of their pasture, they will get lost. Unlike the nursery rhyme, if you leave them alone, they will *not* come home. You will have to go find them. It is best to keep them in a fenced in area. They need more substantial fencing than cattle but take a lot less room.

Seven ewes with their lambs only require as much space as one cow and her heifer. The fencing, can help keep out some predators such as coyotes. It will not kept out bears, wolves or mountain lions. Dogs, donkeys or llamas help protect sheep. Llama wool gets a good price.

In 2018, a *University of California* study said it cost an average of $88 to raise an ewe lamb for market. They are sold when they weigh between 100 to 140 pounds, with the average being 135 pounds. They sell for between $2.50 to $4.00 per pound, with the average selling for $3.25 per pound. That means a 135-pound market ewe sells for about $438.75, yielding an average profit of $350.75 each.

According to the *United States Department of Agriculture's* (USDA) December 2018 bulletin, sheep sell for almost 50% more in Pennsylvania than they do in California or out west.

Sheep are usually sold shorn, minus their wool. You can sell the wool from the sheep. They are usually sheared one time a year and again when sold for meet.

In the United States the average sheep yields 7.3 pounds of wool a year. Sheep in Nevada average about 10.4 pounds per sheep. Wool sells for an average of $0.40 per pound ungraded and $1.00 per pound graded.

Lambs generally end up with a 50 percent carcass weight and 75 percent meat from a carcass. A 135-pound lamb will yield about 50 pounds of meat. That meat in 2018 sold for an average of $12.70 per pound. The profit would be $635 minus the $88 to raise the lamb, giving a profit of $547 per lamb.

You will earn almost $100 more per lamb if you raise and butcher them yourself and sell them for meat than if you just raise and sell them.

104. Raise Goats.

Raising goats for meat or milk can be very productive. You do not need a lot of room or lush fields to raise goats. You can raise them in smaller spaces than sheep.

A large percentage eat goat's meat. I was not raised eating goat but there are some communities where goat is an important part of their diet, such as Muslims and those from the Caribbean.

Goats can also be milked. Some 65 percent of the world's population drink goat milk. Their milk is used to make cheese. My mother was Norwegian and goats milk cheese is often part of a Norwegian diet.

We had a farmer near us who used to raise sheep to sell. One day I notice there weren't any sheep in his fields. I saw him outside and asked if he stopped his sheep business. He told me he started to raise goats instead. He said goats are much easier to raise than sheep. He said you often need to be nearby when sheep deliver their offspring but did not need to be around when goats gave birth.

He told me his biggest market for selling goats was to the Muslim community and to those from the Caribbean. He said they would buy the goats alive because part of their culture is to kill and prepare the goat themselves. He said as soon as a goat was born, he had a buyer who committed to buy that goat when it was old enough to sell.

There is a big market for kid goats. Those are between 3 to 5 months old and weigh between 25 to 30 pounds. Females sell for twice the price of males. You can also sell adult goats.

Many years ago, goats were commonly used for mowing because of the way they eat grass. They were staked in a certain area or let loose in a fenced in area and did their job.

You may want to get some goats and provide an environmentally friendly, all-natural mowing service. You must keep in mind goats will also eat other plants and flowers. You must keep the goats away from anything you do not want them to eat.

Services You Can Sell

There are many tasks people either do not want to do, or ones they cannot do themselves. People will pay someone to provide those services.

Many of these services do not require great skill, though developing greater skill doing any of these will earn you more income.

Some of the services in this section could be done on an as-you-need income basis or could become a regular part-time or full-time job.

Make sure you read the **Important Considerations** section. You may need a business license do some of these.

105. Return Shopping & Luggage Carts.

This is not really a service to sell but a very simple thing you can do to generate a little additional income.

In order to use luggage carts in airports and shopping carts in some stores you must insert coins in a unit attached to the cart. When you finish using the cart, if you return it to the rack some of the coins are refunded to you. Where such a system exists, it is interesting to note many people do not return the carts.

You do not have to be the person who paid to use the cart to return it and get the refund. Some companies hire people to gather up the unreturned carts but if you return those carts, the money becomes yours.

In the movie, *The Terminal,* Tom Hanks character was stuck in an airport for a long period and retrieved enough money to buy all his meals every day.

Some stores require you to pay $0.25 to use a shopping cart. If you return the cart you receive your $0.25 back. That saves the store from hiring an attendant to retrieve the carts, which is a big saving for them. You do not have to be the one who inserted the money to get the refund.

One of our favorite stores, *Aldi*, uses this method. It is not unusual to find an unreturned cart when we go shopping there. My children especially love to return the carts and pocket the money they receive. That certainly is not much money, but it does generate some income.

106. Pass Out or Post Fliers.

Business and politicians often pay people to pass out fliers or brochures. You can do this on the street, in parks, door-to-door and even on some college campuses.

Some people advertise a service where they will post a certain amount of fliers in a city or on a college campus, or put fliers under college or apartment dorm doors. Some even offer a simple printing service.

There is a website called *Fiverr*, where many people

post their services. An average rate for posting or delivering fliers is $10 for 50 brochures. Some add a $10-$20 charge to do it all on one specific day.

Once you develop a reputation as reliable, you will get much more business doing this.

107. Hold Going Out of Business Signs.

Furniture stores and some other companies often have going out of business sales. Sometime the same store goes out of business multiple times. They often pay people to stand along the street and hold their signs. This is an easy way to generate some immediate income.

If you have some special attention getting outfits, you may be able to get more jobs. Gorilla or Alien costumes often go over well and let you disguise yourself while you do this task.

108. Deliver Newspapers.

Delivering and selling newspapers has been a way to generate income for many years. I know children and adults alike who earned income with paper routes for many years. Some deliver newspapers before they go to their regular job to generate additional income. Some deliver papers only on weekends.

Newspaper publishers need people to deliver their newspapers. That can be done with a bicycle, car, or truck. It can be done on horseback, by dogsled or on foot. Some also sell newspapers on the street like the *Newsies* of old.

Newsies is am inspiring Disney Musical and Broadway show about the struggle the newspaper boys faced in in New York City at the beginning of the twentieth-century.

My family was in the newspaper business. My great grandfather, John H. Maxwell I, worked as a reporter and printing press operator in New York City. He helped start the first printer's union. It was a very powerful union. Its members were part of powerful political force known as *Tammany Hall*, which influenced elections in the city.

John Maxwell was the Vice-President of *Tammany Hall*.

I worked as a reporter and news correspondent for a daily and a weekly newspaper and also for the *United Press International* (UPI), a major news service.

109. Make Phone Calls.

Many companies and politicians hire people to make phone calls for them. You either work out of an office, a call center, or in some cases you can work from home.

Most companies pay an hourly rate for this work. Some also pay commissions.

There is a lot of turnover of people in this field so there are often many opportunities for work.

You do not really need any abilities to do this one, other than the ability to talk on a phone. Many places have a basic format or script for you to follow when you make calls.

If you know another language that can expand your opportunities.

The more pleasant or persuasive you are, the more job opportunities you will find.

110. Mow Lawns.

Mowing lawns has always been a simple method for earning money. You can do one or two lawns and generate a little income or do as many as your schedule allows.

When I was in grade school I started mowing lawns for others. Unlike others, I did not charge a specific amount. I told people to pay me what they thought the job was worth. I always made more than anyone who set a specific price.

You may be able to generate some immediate income by looking for some homes which need mowing, and then offering them your service.

If you do this as a regular business you may need a permit or license. See the **Important Considerations** section at the end of this book.

You must be extra careful when you mow other people's lawns. Most people expect you not to run over their flowers. Most expect you to do some trimming as well as mowing. Many expect you to remove the grass which is cut down. You should ask if they have a place for that.

Some more environmentally conscious people may allow you to use a mulch mower, which cuts the grass small and does not need to be removed.

111. Do Yard Work.

Many people need some yard work done, other than mowing. This could include *spring clean-up*, which must take place before someone starts regular mowing.

This could also include weeding, trimming trees or bushes, and raking leaves in the fall. It could also include doing some planting.

You may be able to find some jobs doing this with an online service such as *TaskRabbit*. People contact them with jobs needing to be done. When you are available to do some work, you look at *TaskRabbit* to see if anyone needs work done. You get paid directly by the online service.

112. Cut Down Trees.

People charge a lot of money to cut down trees. If you have a good chain saw and a pick-up truck or small trailer you may be able to earn some significant money doing this.

When five tornadoes hit our area this year, many people were shocked to learn the price to remove one fallen tree was more than $1,000 to as high as $10,000. Some people received so much work removing trees they bought new equipment and paid it off with that one storm.

113. Sell Firewood.

Many people use firewood. Some cut it down themselves, but more people pay someone else to provide them with wood.

To make money with this method you need a source for wood, a way to split that wood, and a way to deliver the split wood to customers.

Years ago, people cut down trees with axes and saws. They then split the wood with an axe. That was hard work. Now most people use chain saws and gas-powered wood splitters to do the job.

It is important to know, you can cut down trees, but you cannot sell them for firewood right away. They need to dry for a season first, so they burn better.

When I lived in New Hampshire we had a house with a wood stove. I learned different species of wood produce different amounts of heat. I was told apple and cherry burn extra hot and to never fill my stove with one of those woods but to mix them with others.

I was told to never use pine in my woodstove because it generates a significant amount of *creosote* in the chimney, which can cause dangerous chimney fires.

When I was in Utah I stayed at a place that heated with wood. I asked what kind of wood they used. They said they used pine. I was surprised and told them I was told that was not safe. They said that was the only wood they had in their area. They said they had to clean their chimneys more often because of the *creosote* build-up.

To have a source for wood and to maximize your earning potential you may be able to combine a tree cutting service with a firewood business.

Some towns have road crews or power companies who cut down trees near power lines. Some leave the cut down wood by the side of the road and welcome people to remove it. Some crews take the wood back to a location where it is chipped. Some of those places welcome people who come take the wood.

After the five tornadoes hit our area, thousands of trees were blown down and blocked roads for days. For months many people gladly paid people to come cut up their wood and take it away. Some people cut up the wood and left it near the road with signs saying *Free Firewood*.

In areas where there are campgrounds or cabins many local people cut up and sell small bundles of wood to generate some additional income.

114. Set Up Generators.

If you live in an area where there are power outages you may be able to generate some income setting up generators for people.

When power goes out most people have no power for lights or for their televisions to work. That alone upsets some people. Though that is inconvenient there are potentially life-threatening consequences such as no electric for heat or air conditioning. In many places there will be no water, which also means no water to replenish a flushed toilet. People dependent on home medical equipment can end up in a dangerous situation.

In areas where there are storms which cause outages many people and businesses secure back-up generators. Many of them have no idea how to properly set them up.

After some people use a gasoline powered generator and find the difficulties associated with that, many want to switch to a propane powered back-up generator hooked up to their home power box. That way all they have to do when there is a power outage is to flip a switch.

There are two mistakes people often make with generators. The first one is if you use a gasoline powered generator, you must start it periodically or it will not start when you need it. That is very frustrating. Propane generators do not have that problem.

As a fireman I learned the second mistake people make. When there is an outage and they use a generator hooked up to their house many people do not turn off the switch bringing electric into the house. The problem with that is the power from the generator back feeds into the outside power lines. People touching those wires, thinking there is no power in them, can get hurt.

115. Help People Set Up Composting.

Composting is an environmentally responsible thing to do but most people have no idea how to do it. You may be able to generate additional income by helping people set up composting.

If you live in a densely populated area, where there are many lawns if you can get people to compost, that will provide a good way to consolidate grass clippings and leaves and put them to work helping the environment.

You may put together a simple composting package which people can order through you and which you come and personally setup.

116. Shovel Snow or Clean Off Cars.

If you live in an area where it snows, this can be a fast way to make some immediate income. Carry a snow shovel or snow brush with you and offer to help others.

Most municipalities require residents and businesses to keep their sidewalks free from snow and ice. Some smaller stores would rather pay you to do this task than to have one of their employees do it.

When it snows, people coming out of work, or shopping, or at a train station greatly appreciate help brushing snow off their car or shoveling them out. You do not have to charge anything, just offer to help. Most people will give you something for helping. Sometimes the amount they give will be more than you would receive if you charged a certain amount.

If you plan to shovel walkways or driveways, I personally recommend a *snow scoop* or *sleigh shovel*. These are a Canadian invention. They hold a lot of snow and are very easy to use. You just push them, and they work like a plow.

You may also consider doing snow shoveling or snow plowing for a snow shoveling service like *Shovler* or a snow plowing service like *SnoHub*. During snowy weather, people contact the service and tell them where they are and the size of the area where they need the snow removed. You check in with the service and get your assignment. You do the job, the service collects the money, and pays you digitally. I know one man who uses such a service and follows a snow storm through a few states making a significant amount of money in a few days.

117. Wash Windows & Power Wash.

Washing windows has been a way to generate income for many years. All businesses and homes have many windows which get dirty. Most people do not want to take the time to wash windows and will pay someone else.

You may be surprised how many people in your area have not washed their windows for years and would gladly pay you to do that task.

All you need to provide window washing service is a bucket, water, cleaner, squeegee, a rag and maybe a ladder.

Some people combine a window washing and home power washing service to maximize their income. That only requires the addition of a power washer. It is easier and faster to power wash a house and wash the windows at the same time. You just need to have a good power washer and learn the proper settings. If you do this wrong you may end up stripping paint off a house and breaking some windows.

A power washer can also be used for cleaning and stripping wood decking, which should be done at least every other year.

You can provide this service to businesses and homeowners. If you do a good job these services tend to generate repeat customers.

Gas powered power washers are more powerful than electric ones. If you use electric ones you need a power source, which might require a generator, making the gas powered one the better choice.

118. Take Out & Return Trash Cans.

Many people do not like to take out or return their trash cans. If you do that for them, you may be able to generate some additional income.

If people have an outside place where they keep their trash receptacles you may offer to take out their trash containers and then return the empty trash cans later.

If they do not have an outside storage place for their trash cans, you still may be able to provide a service bringing their trash cans up from the road to their house. This may seem like a very small task, but it is one some people will greatly appreciate.

This is a very simple service. If you have the time, and secure enough customers, you could charge a minimal amount for this service and still generate steady income.

119. Provide Removal of Larger Items.

Many times, people have large things they need help disposing of. This is especially true after a storm does damage or a person passes away.

Some of the more common larger items needing removal are old furniture, appliances, old riding mowers and pianos. Sometimes this could involve removing old playground equipment, old vehicles and debris for construction or remodeling.

Some people may want help disposing of an unwanted relative but that is a different matter usually handled by other people.

Unless you are a very large and very strong person this method usually works best with a co-worker. You also need a pick-up truck, box truck, van, or small trailer to remove larger items. You may be able to rent one of those.

You also need a place to take the items you remove. You may be able to resell some of the items you remove, or you may be able to sell them for scrap.

You may have to pay to dispose of the items. Be sure to

include that cost in your removal price.

120. Clean Homes.

For many years people generated additional income cleaning homes for others. Some do it part-time some do it full-time.

There are many cleaning services you maybe be able to work for or you may be able to do this on your own.

You will get more business if you, and the vehicle you drive, look professional. If you wear dark clothing and sunglasses, and always look over your shoulder when people talk with you, you probably will not get many jobs.

Some people provide a service cleaning up apartments and houses after tenants move out. I did that in college.

Some clean vacation and seasonal rentals, especially for absentee landowners. My brother John did that in New Hampshire.

Make sure to get a list of the tasks a client wants accomplished. Then go over that with them in person, if possible.

121. Clean Offices.

Cleaning offices is similar to cleaning houses. This is usually done after business hours at night or on weekends.

I had a pastor friend in New Hampshire who did this part-time and generated more income doing this than he received from his small church.

122. Provide a Laundry Service.

This is a method of generating income which people have provided for thousands of years. You may be able to earn money doing laundry for others.

People need their clothing washed and many people hate to wash clothes. This is especially true of single working parents, college students, some seniors, and most other people I know.

Some people provide a service where they pick up clothing, wash it and return it. Others provide this service in a person's home using their washing machine and dryer.

You may also be able to provide this service to some small local businesses that need laundry done, like restaurants, garages, factories, or schools.

You may be able to provide an inhouse laundry service as a sub-contractor to a local hotel or motel saving the expense of hiring additional personnel.

123. Provide a Diaper Washing Service.

Most people use disposable diapers for their babies. The problem is those disposable diapers are filling up landfills. Some people are becoming more concerned about the environment and would use cloth diapers if there was a diaper washing service available.

In 1961, the first disposable diapers were introduced to the market. In 1970, 350,000 tons of disposable diapers ended up in landfills. By 1980, that number climbed to 1.9 million tons per year. By 2006, that number almost doubled to 3.6 million tons. By 2007, the age of children wearing disposable diapers greatly expanded with many wearing them up through five years of age.

It is estimated it will take until the year 2500 for those disposable diapers to degrade. Many people are becoming more aware and concerned about this environmental challenge. Surveys show 7 out of 10 people favor banning disposable diapers.

Legislation to ban disposable diapers has been introduced in many municipalities. This is creating the potential for some people to generate some very significant income with a diaper washing service.

When I was growing up our family used a lot of cloth diapers. I had two siblings older than me and two who were younger. In addition to that we often had two foster babies. I changed hundreds of diapers. The soiled cloth diapers were rinsed in the toilet, then place in a diaper hamper, and then washed. I hated the whole affair.

We had neighbors who used a diaper washing service. Today, you may be able to set-up such a service. It usually involves picking up soiled diapers and dropping off clean ones at the same time.

The average diaper services provide a choice of diapers and do a weekly pick-up and delivery. The average cost is $18-$24 per week, depending on where you live.

Most services provide an airtight pail, air fresheners, liner, and waterproof outer layer to be worn with the diapers. Some services require people to rinse off the diapers in their toilet before placing them in the pail.

Baby diapers require more than a standard rinse and wash cycle to properly sanitize them.

If you provide such a service determine how many diapers you want to handle. Newborns to 5 months old use an average of 10 diapers a day, which is about 70 per week. From 5 months old to 12 months most average 8 diapers per day resulting in a total of 56 per week.

If you have 5 customers whose children were about ½ newborns and ½ older ones you would average washing about 315 diapers a week. Depending on your washing machine, you could wash 32 diapers per load. That means it would take about 10 loads to wash those 315 diapers. Some recommend a 30-minute pre-rinse, 15-minute agitation cycle plus two rinse cycles at the end. That takes about a total of 118 minutes per load. That means it would take you about 20 hours at 2 hours per load x 10 loads.

This is a stinky, labor intensive, often very low paying way to generate income, but it provides a needed service and it helps the environment.

124. Take Pictures of Events.

Some people love to take pictures. In my lifetime the picture taking industry has changed dramatically. When I was young you had to go to a nearby cave and find someone with artistic ability who owned a hammer and chisel. You would sit there for a few days while they would carve your image on your cave wall. Sometimes they would carve out images of your favorite dinosaur hunt.

Then came the invention of the camera and film. That changed everything. We no longer had to pose for pictures for days. The photographed placed a plate in the back of a big box with a lens and you only had to sit still for a minute or so, to have your picture taken, and then wait for the film to be developed and pictures printed.

Improvements in cameras came quickly. Film came on rolls and pictures could be taken in a matter of seconds. You then sent the film off to be processed and printed. Or you could take it to some small businesses that looked like outhouses which provided that service.

During that last phase I worked as a photographer for the newspapers. I took a camera and three or four rolls of black and white film to an event. The cameras I used were more expensive than the average person owned. I had to control the speed and opening of the lens to get good pictures. I would shoot as many pictures as possible and then drive them back to the newspaper office. Once I arrived, I would bring the film to the developing room where they would develop the film while I worked on writing the story to go with the pictures.

Then came the digital age. Anyone with a digital camera or smart phone can now take potentially high-quality pictures and have them instantly ready to view.

You may want to consider getting a drone with a camera, so you can take pictures from some more interesting angles.

Put together a portfolio of pictures you took which get published. You can use that to get more work.

Ways to Make Money with Event Photos:

Sell Photos to Newspapers

Newspapers use professional photographers but also use pictures submitted by average people.

Photographers from newspapers cannot be at every news worthy event. All you have to do is be at an event, takes some pictures and send them to a newspaper right away. Some papers will pay you for those pictures.

Daily newspapers like action photos, photos of celebrities, or photos which capture great expressions on people's faces. That is how I started taking pictures. That led to my work with a daily paper and then with the *United Press International* (UPI).

You can start by taking pictures for local papers. They are much less demanding than daily papers and need pictures and stories. They love pictures of local events, social gatherings, local sporting events and groups of people.

Make sure you identify the names of all the people in the photographs.

If you take good pictures and submit them right away, you can create a demand for your work and can generate more income.

Sell Photos to Stock Photo Companies

Stock photo companies buy photographs to resell.

Sell Photos Online

You can also take pictures at events and offer them for sale on *Facebook* or on a website. Many people who attend events love to have pictures of themselves.

If you want to earn money this way make sure you place a very obvious watermark on the photos, so people will not want to download them and print them without paying you for them.

125. Take Pictures of Businesses.

Local businesses need pictures to promote their business. If you can take good pictures you may be able to generate some extra income doing this.

One way to start doing this is to pick one of your

favorite local businesses and ask them if you can take some pictures. Then take a lot of pictures of that business. Take both candid and posed pictures with happy people in the pictures. Make sure you take pictures of some of the special features of the business and of employees in action.

After you take the pictures, go through them, and pick the best ones. Print them and possibly frame one or two. Then show them to the owner of the business. Let them know they can use those pictures to promote their business. Those pictures could be used in fliers or advertisements.

Be sure to include a poor man's copyright on each picture, which includes: the word Copyright, the year, your name, and the words, All Rights Reserved.

Put together a portfolio of the photos you take and bring them to a local newspaper or local ad agency to show them your work. That may get you some business.

126. Take Pictures of People.

Most people like to see pictures which include themselves, their family, their friends, their pets, their home, and things they care about. That can help you generate some additional income.

Though many people have their own cameras or phones which can take pictures, many tourist attractions learned there is a good market taking pictures of other people and offering them for sale. Some places have paid photographers on location who take pictures of people, which they in turn offer for sale.

Though people can take selfies, or pictures of people with them, those usually are not as good as pictures taken of them by someone else.

There are many ways you can generate additional income taking pictures of other people. You can take instant pictures of people or take pictures you post on a website they can buy. Many people will not go look online for a picture you took, so you are more likely to do better selling instant pictures for some of these methods.

To do instant pictures you need either a good quality instant film camera or you need to have a good quality portable inkjet printer with you.

Instant picture technology has changed significantly over the years. Years ago, people took pictures of people with the original *Polaroid* cameras and sold those. There are better quality instant cameras available now. Many take very small pictures, but some will take a 3"x5" picture. That is a better size for selling.

The problem with instant pictures is they are expensive. Unlike a traditional camera, with an instant camera, you do not want to take more than one picture of a subject if you want to make money.

Some methods for taking pictures allow more time to provide prints so you do not have to use an instant camera.

Take Pictures of People at Local Sites

If there are any historic or tourist sites in your area you may want to go there and offer a service taking pictures of people. That can also work well at beaches.

Do not try to take pictures hiding behind trees or in a disguise. Wear a shirt or vest identifying you as a photographer. Also wear a name tag and if possible, have a sign you display when you take pictures.

Always ask people before you take their picture.

If you are at a managed site you may not be able to take pictures to resell unless you contact management. You may offer your services as a photographer and work out a deal where they allow you to take pictures. You may offer to pay the site a set amount per photo sold.

Take Pictures of People at Events

People love to have good pictures of them at an event.

You may need to work out an agreement with an event organizer.

You could offer this service taking pictures of people

with celebrities at events. You may be able to charge to take a picture of people with a celebrity using their own camera. The fee would be split between you and the celebrity or event organizer.

Take Pictures of People's Homes

Many people like to have nice pictures of their homes. Professionals have provided that service for years.

You can take pictures of people's homes or of people in front of their home.

It is a good idea to get practice doing this by taking pictures of your home or of your friend's homes.

Some people offer aerial photographs of homes. They tend to be very pricy. They do it will periodic fly-overs in an airplane. If you invest in a drone you might be able to take some nice aerial photos.

If you take good pictures you may offer this as a service to local real estate agents.

Take Pictures of Local Teams

You can take pictures of local sports teams in action. You may also be able to offer to take a team and individual photos.

127. Make Slide/Image Shows.

Many people love to see slide/image shows of family members. This is especially appreciated for funerals and memorial services. You may be able to provide this meaningful service.

This often requires a quick turn-around time.

One way to do this is to put together a slide/image show, with photos provided by the family, which they can use at a funeral or memorial service.

You can offer this on a flash drive which can be used on a television at a funeral home or may want to offer a complete package with a television screen and stand.

You can also provide this as a nice service for people in

the hospital and especially for people in hospice.

When *Lady Jane*, the wife of our local sheriff was in hospice, her son put together a slide show with many pictures of family, events, and scenery, along with some nice music. It played on a television in his mother's room for days. It provided comfort for her and all who visited. She told me how much she appreciated it. The hospice facility said they would love it for everyone did something like that for their patients.

You can provide a service like this for local businesses. You take pictures and put together a slide/image show which plays on a loop on a television in their waiting room or for a trade show or event.

128. Do Digital Photo Conversion.

Many people have photographs, slides, negatives, and film which they would love to have digitized and preserved.

This can be done with some specialized equipment or with a simple home-made set-up.

Some method of digitizing and saving pictures have turned out not to be as permanent as once thought. It is best to save your work in at least two different formats.

129. Do Genealogy for Others.

Many people are interested in their family background. The study of a person's ancestry is known as *genealogy*. The person who studies genealogy is called a *genealogist*.

Years ago, you had to hire a professional genealogist to do your genealogy. It was quite expensive.

Many families officially or unofficially designated someone to serve as the family historian. They were the one you went to when you wanted to know about your family background. Most of the people who did that work were very sincere. Some were sincerely right, and some were sincerely wrong. Some did it quite well, some did not.

Some omitted unflattering parts of the family story and others embellished it. There are many good genealogies and many unreliable genealogies out there.

I have been a genealogist for more than 40 years. During that time, I have seen the good, the bad, and the ugly. I have disproved many family myths and found many family gems. You can learn to do that.

Some of the greatest resources I have discovered to assist genealogists have come from the *Church of Jesus Christ of the Latter-Day Saints*, known to many as the *Mormons*. Genealogy plays an important part in their belief system. That is both good and bad. It is good because they preserved records which are now lost. It was bad because some people fudged their genealogies, so they could qualify for some of the church ordinances. The good thing is the Church recognized that and took steps to remedy that. They are the leaders in the field of genealogy.

When I started doing genealogy the internet did not have any of the resources available today. I had to physically go from town to town to physically find records. I was so glad when I discovered that *Latter-Day Saints Family History Libraries* and *United States Archives Regional Centers* had microfilms of many documents, especially census records.

Over the years, I made trips to the *Family History Library* in Salt Lake City, Utah to study microfilms and other records. Back then, many of them were not indexed.

I was thrilled when people began to index the films. That save me hundreds of hours or work. Then I was elated when records began to be posted on the internet.

There are so many records on the internet, which can be accessed for free , which are extremely helpful to genealogists, such as Census records. You can also find immigration records on the *Ellis Island* website.

Some companies, such as *Ancestry* offer a combination of invaluable free and subscription-based services online. Some libraries like our local *Patterson Library* and the

Mid-Hudson Library System provide many of those resources for free to their patrons.

If you learn how to do basic genealogy you can generate income doing family trees for people. If you develop more skills you may be able to generate even more income.

130. Tune Bicycles.

Most people know a car periodically needs a tune-up. I was surprised when I learned bicycles also need tune-ups. A well-tuned bicycle provides a better ride and will often last longer than an untuned one.

Two of my brothers worked in bicycle shops. One of them accompanied cross-country bicycle trips repairing and tuning up the bicycles.

If you learn how to tune-up bicycles you may be able to generate some extra income. You can find videos on *YouTube* showing you how to do this.

131. Detail Cars.

Many people like to keep their cars looking new. To do that requires more than just washing the outside of the vehicle. Detailing a car cleans both the outside and inside of a car so it looks as new as possible.

You may be able to generate additional income detailing cars for people. It is not a difficult skill to learn. I knew a homeless man who generated income detailing cars for people. Doing one car a week provided all the food he needed. You do not need to be homeless to do this.

There are people who provide a detailing service which comes and detail people's cars while they work. That can be a very profitable business.

You could take this a step further and do what Zeke Hubbard did. I met Zeke in New Hampshire. He was working on a *Mercedes Benz* sportscar for someone. He totally refinished the car outside and inside. He said the person he was doing the work for was not in a rush, so he took his time doing the job. He told me he was paid $25,000 for the job.

132. Do Make-Overs.

You may be able to generate income doing make overs for other people. A make-over is where you help someone transform the way they look. It can include a change of clothing, hairstyle, or make-up.

The saying, *you cannot judge a book by its cover*, is good advice but many people do judge books and people by the way they look. The way we look and the clothing we wear can affect how others perceive us, either for good or for bad.

Shakespeare said, *"apparel oft proclaims the man."*

Two other says are true, *beauty is only skin deep*, and *beauty is in the eye of the beholder*. You should not be obsessed with how you look but there is nothing wrong with trying to look your best.

The way we look can also affect the way we think about ourselves. Many people like to look good. Though *looking good* does not mean someone is good, when people think they look good that often helps them feel good about themselves. It can even help them act better. That is one reason many parochial schools and businesses have dress codes.

I have seen the look on people's faces change when they wear an outfit they think makes them look good, or when they leave the barber shop or beauty salon.

Many actors, models and politicians hire people to help them look good. Sometimes the change they accomplish is drastic. I have been shocked to see the transformation in some before and after pictures of certain people.

There have been numerous make-over shows on television where people are selected for a makeover. That usually includes a change of wardrobe and hair style. For women, it always includes showing them how to wear make-up in a way that compliments or enhances their natural beauty.

If you can do a good job helping people with make-overs you may be able to generate some significant money.

Make sure you keep a *before and after* portfolio of your work.

133. Do Clothing Consulting.

Have you ever heard the saying, *clothing make the man*? Some countered with, *the man makes the clothing*. I believe the truth is half way between those statements.

Some people earn income helping people select clothing. This is different than a make-over. Here you help people determine what clothing they should wear for specific or different occasions.

This is good place to insert an important word of advice I learned many years ago. Learn how to compliment people. Many people do not do this well.

The following two statements are compliments. Consider the difference between them.

That outfit looks amazing.

That outfit looks amazing on you.

Often we mean well when we compliment someone, but our choice of words may not be the best. The words we use are important. The first statement, *that outfit looks amazing*, compliments the person's choice of the outfit. It does not compliment the person.

The second statement, *that outfit looks amazing on you*, could possibly be complimenting the choice of the outfit but it goes much farther. It complements the way the outfit looks on that person. That outfit might not look amazing on someone else. That is the better compliment.

I help sponsor a Boys Scout Venture Crew. They have a clothing collection box in our town. At different times of the year they pick out coats to help people in the city. They also pick out dress clothing which is used to help people look better when they go for a job interview. The way a person dresses for a job interview is very important.

I knew some top executives who worked for IBM. Their company had a strict clothing policy everyone was familiar with. When Thomas J. Watson, the founder of the company, was seeking to fill an executive position he invited the prospective employee to the IBM Country Club, along with their spouse and children. What the prospect did not understand was, they were being judged by what the wore. Watson felt it was important what an executive, who would be representing his company, wore both to the office and in a casual setting.

People usually select clothing they think looks good. Sometimes that clothing looks good on them, sometimes it does not. Some people understand that and want their clothing to look good on them and to communicate the right message for the right occasion. Some know they are not the best person to make those decisions. A clothing consultant helps them select the right outfits that look good on them for the right occasions.

The clothing does not have to be expensive for it to look good. One day, while I was working as an executive for a successful company, I noticed one of the more important people in the company was wearing a suit which looked just like mine. He also noticed that and asked me how I was able to afford such an expensive suit. I just smiled and replied, *I think it is important to look good for work.* I did not tell him I bought the suit at a factory outlet store. That suit normally retailed for $599, I bought it for $99.

134. Be a Personal Shopper.

Many companies have Purchasing Agents whose role is to buy supplies, equipment, services, and other supplies. My brother Frank has been a Purchasing Agent for hospitals for many years. He is good at his job and his employers view him as a valuable employee.

There is an opportunity and need for people to be Purchasing Agents in the private sector. In the private sector they are sometimes called *Personal Shoppers.*

Some people are either too busy to shop, do not like to shop, or realize other people can do a better job shopping for specific items. That has created the opportunity for you to be a Personal Shopper. You can provide one or more of these services to one or more people. This can be a small casual income generating endeavor or it could become a full-scale significant business.

The role of a Personal Shopper is to determine what someone needs or wants and to then locate that item for them at the best price.

There are various services you can provide as a Personal Shopper. Some are more focused and require a more specific skill set which you must have or acquire.

In my book, *More Than 500 Proven Ways to Reduce Expenses*, I address how to find good buys for some of these services. I recommend you read that book and apply those methods to help you be a better Personal Shopper.

For some of these services you need to be in the same geographic area as the people for whom you provide the service. For many of these services you can be in a different area and conduct your business online or by phone.

It is a good idea to keep a list of satisfied customers and put together a portfolio of the work you accomplished.

The first time you provide one of these services will take you the most amount of time. The more you provide any of these services, you will develop a database of more contact and resources and it will take you less time.

Shopping for Necessities

This is the easiest category, yet most overlooked service, a Personal Shopper can provide. People need household supplies and food. You find the best buys and arrange the purchase and delivery of those items.

This is especially helpful when provided as a local service to senior citizens or shut-ins.

Shopping for Technology

Most people want technology, such as cell phones,

computers, printers, etc. Yet many do not really know what they need or how to find the best buys. They often spend too much money and regret what they bought.

If you are good at this, you can help people get what they want and need for the best price. You do not sell the equipment or software, you just charge a fee to help them get what they need. One happy customer will bring many others.

To do this effectively, you need to keep up on the latest trends and places to find the best buys.

Shopping for Cars

Too many people spend too much money when they buy a car. I have a friend Joe Downey who runs *Downey Motors* in Pawling, New York. Joe is a great trustworthy auto mechanic and sells quality used cars. If Joe does not have a car in stock, which someone needs or wants, he tries to locate one for his customer.

It helps to be a mechanic to do this, but that is not necessary. You may be good at finding good deals on cars and can generate some extra income doing this

Shopping for Clothing

Everyone needs clothing. If you learn the techniques for saving money when you buy clothing you may be able to offer that as a service to others. You could locate the best buys on new or used clothing.

Shopping for Gifts

Gift buying services have been around for more than 100 years. Most people want to give a good meaningful gift to others. The problem is many people do not know what to get for someone.

Your role is to learn the best gift for someone and then find it at the best price.

The most important part is discovering what gift will be appreciated by an individual. For some gift givers, that is more important the amount of money they spend.

Shopping for Furniture & Home Decor

Many people make a living as an Interior Decorator or Designer. They help people determine what they want in their home. Some help secure those items.

Some people have a natural eye for this. Perhaps you are one of those people.

Once you determine what someone wants or needs, you need to determine if those items need to be new, custom-made or if they can be vintage items. Items such as beds should obviously be new. Furniture and home décor can often be vintage.

Many decorators and designers find their buys at thrift shops and flea markets.

Shopping for Art & Collectables

Many items fall under art and collectibles. It could be paintings, sculptures, pottery, historical artifacts, militaria, coins, jewels, trading cards, stamps, and many other items.

Many people love art and collectibles and will pay a significant amount of money to secure items they desire. If you have an interest in this and can develop the right skills, you may be able to generate significant income helping people find art or collectibles.

I have a friend, Jonathan Ohara, who runs an art gallery in New York City. He is a skilled art buyer. He has an eye for quality art and is very experienced helping people secure what they want or need. That is a skill people appreciate.

The prices of art and collectibles varies greatly and frequently fluctuates. You need to know when and where to buy.

You must know the difference between authentic and reproduction items. I did graduate work in document examination and handwriting authentication. I find that helpful in determining the authenticity of a document or signature. You may need to secure the help of someone which such skills in the course of doing business.

Shopping for Travel

Many people like to travel but end up spending too much money for what they get. Some plan their vacations by themselves and end up dissatisfied with their accommodations. That gave rise to the Travel Agent and to agencies which provide travel services, such as *AAA (American Automobile Association)*.

There are travel guides and numerous websites which provide travel services. Those can be a big help planning a vacation, but you must be careful. Some travel publications give higher recommendations to the providers who advertise with them. We encountered that one year when we traveled across the United States. We put our trust in the reviews in one of those publications and booked accommodations in New Orleans. We arrived late at night to find the place was in an industrial district . There were pimps, prostitutes, and homeless people hanging around outside. The swimming pool turned out to be so small not even six people could fit inside of it. It was awful. We realized we could not trust that travel guide and threw it away.

Travel agents are paid a commission on the accommodations they book. Some are great and can help people have a wonderful vacation. Many travel providers give special deals to travel agents to come check out their accommodations, so they can recommend them to others. I have a friend, Susan Rebentisch, who did that when she worked as a travel agent. She visited locations and carefully checked out accommodations, so she could better serve her clients.

My mother did some work as a travel agent. My brother Frank and I went with her on a group trip to Switzerland. She booked incredible accommodations at a nice chalet. We skied from the chalet down to a bus each day and then travelled around Interlaken. I met some people who paid $2,000 more than the price the people in my mother's tour paid, and those other people told me they had inferior accommodations.

I learned how to book my own flights and accommodations and saved hundreds of dollars. In my travels I often discover the person sitting in the seat next to me in the airplane paid much for than I did.

You may be able to generate some extra income helping people with their travel arrangements.

Shopping for Books

You may be able to generate additional income by providing a book buying service. Your job is to find people the books they want at the best price.

Many people like to read but often pay too much for books because they do not know where to find the best buys. Many have some favorite authors and want to read every book written by them. Some of those books are hard to find, if you do not know where to look.

One of the best sites for locating books is *Amazon.com*. Most people do not know how to use that site and often pay too much for books. For example, *Ingram* released my book, *Sybil Rides: The Female Paul Revere, The Burning of Danbury and Battle of Ridgefield*, on *Amazon.com* for $19.95. The first printing sold out in two weeks. On the third week I searched for my book on *Amazon.com* and the search feature took me to the book and showed the selling price as $34.95. That was being sold by a third-party reseller who marked-up the book, even though they did not have any copies. There were some other purchase options listed, but you would not find them unless you saw the small print with that link. The book was still available for $19.95. As I am writing this, one person has a used copy of my book listed on *Amazon.com* for $292!

Many people do not understand the *Other New and Used Copies* feature on *Amazon.com*. When you do a search for a book there is often the option in small print which shows *Other New and Used Copies* of the book.

If you click that link you will often discover *new* or *like new* copies of the same book for much less than the first link you arrived at. Some of the *like new* copies are new copies of the book which have sat on a shelf and look just as good as copies direct from the publisher. The listings will tell you the condition. You can often save a significant amount of money.

If you do a *Google* search, you may discover lower cost options. My daughter wanted an out of print book. On *Amazon.com* and *eBay* the book sold for hundreds of dollars. Using *Google,* I found a copy for $20.

135. Provide an On-Site Shredding Service.

Many people have documents with important information they do not want others to see. There are notorious people who sort through documents looking for important personal or financial information they can use to their advantage. That gave rise to the paper shredder, and then to shredding services.

You may be able to provide an on-site shredding service to some small businesses or individuals in your area. You just need to be trustworthy, own a good quality shredder and have a flexible schedule.

136. Provide a Courier Service.

Would you like to be paid to travel? Consider being a courier. You can do this, travel free, and earn some income at the same time. This can be a very good way to generate additional income.

You can do this working for a courier company, as a sub-contractor, or as an independent courier. Many companies and individuals want things delivered in person by a trustworthy person and may pay you to be their courier. There are opportunities to do this locally, regionally, cross-country, or internationally.

Make sure you have a passport and any necessary visas so you can return home. Make sure your inoculations are up to date.

One way to earn more money is to be a courier to more dangerous area. Those assignments often pay more.

Be careful what you are transporting or you may end up with a very long vacation in a government run facility.

There are professional associations for people who want to be casual international couriers. They provide connections with reputable companies and offer greatly reduced airfare in exchange for carrying documents or items for them. The savings are often 50-85% of what you would normally pay to fly.

The *United States Department of State* hires people every year to serve as diplomatic couriers. They currently pay $38,394-$56,383. They provide tax-free housing overseas, health care, and educational benefits for dependent children.

137. Do Vacation Transport.

You may be able to earn money doing vacation transport. What you do is drive a vehicle for someone else, or for a company, from one location to another.

There are many opportunities for vacation transport. If you just drive a car or motorhome, you do not need a special license.

You may want to consider doing this in the fall, when many senior citizens from the north head south for the winter and need drivers. You can do this in the spring, when they return north.

138. Be a Salvation Army Bell Ringer.

Around the holiday season the Salvation Army solicits funds to help their outreach programs. They often have people stand in front of stores ringing bells, standing next to a donation kettle.

Though some organizations provide volunteers to help the Salvation Army solicit funds they can never get enough volunteers, so they hire people to be bell ringers. They do not pay very well but it is an immediate source of income.

This is usually seasonal work and can put you outside in nasty weather, but some inside opportunities may be available in some shopping malls.

If you play an instrument or dress up as Santa and smile you will get more donations. You will not make more money, but you will be helping more people.

139. Be a Pet Walker.

If you live in a city you may see people walking down the street with numerous dogs on leashes. Those people are often paid dog walkers. That is one way you may be able to generate some additional income.

There are many people who have pets which need to be walked during the day while they are at work. Usually it is dogs which need walking. That provides them an opportunity to relieve themselves and to get some needed exercise and socialization.

When I was growing up we almost always had a dog. All of those dogs needed to be walked. Back then, when you walked a dog they would often *do their business*. Doing their business did not mean they sold things or did banking, though it did involve them leaving a *deposit*. Back then, you just left that *deposit* wherever it was made. Times have changed. Most towns and cities no longer allow you to leave the *deposit*, you must go prepared to scoop poop.

There have been many innovations in the scooping poop business over the years. Find a solution which works best for you.

Some people walk more than one pet at a time. If you want to walk more than one pet at a time make sure they are compatible and that you can handle them.

Perhaps you want to get a cat and give the cat a longer leash and then walk a few dogs behind the cat That could provide both you and the pets with a lot of exercise.

140. Be a Pet Sitter.

Pet Sitting does not mean you sit on pets, though they may end up sitting on you. Pet Sitting is a service where you take care of pets while people are gone. You either visit the pets and take care of them one or more times a day or you stay with them or they stay with you.

There are a wide variety of pets which need care while their owners are gone. Dogs and cats are the most common however there are many others. That can include fish, turtles, birds, snakes, hamsters, mice, rats, alligators, lions, tigers, and bears, oh my!

A good pet sitter does more than just see that a pet is feed. Being apart from one's pet can be a traumatic experience for both the family and the pet. Some pets may wonder if they have been abandoned. A good pet sitter provides not only food but emotional support for pets in the family's absence.

The best way to do this, for the pets physical and emotional well-being, is to go to people's homes to feed and take care of their pets there.

Some people send their pets to a kennel when they are gone. I always thought pet kennels look like pet prisons to me. I wonder what the pets think? I imagine many of them who have to stay in such places, when a family goes on vacation, must feel like they have been abandoned.

Pet sitting in a person's home is not only best for a pet's emotional well-being, it is also less expensive for you as you do not need to provide facilities.

It is usually best to start pet sitting for people and pets you know. If you do not know the pets you are going to be sitting for, try to meet them and get to know them a little before you sit for them. That way the pets will come to know you and may feel more comfortable with you.

Make sure you know the pet's dietary requirements and monitor their feeding habits and their overall health. Some animals will get depressed or be anxious when their family is gone and that can affect their health.

Some pets may need some exercise or need to be taken for a walk. You may need to take them outside to chase the mailman. Make sure they do not run away while you are providing this care.

Always be very careful with any animals for which you provide care. Make sure you know what to do in case of an emergency. Know who the family wants you to contact, such as a veterinarian.

It would be nice if you take pictures periodically of the pets you are caring for while the family is gone, showing they are happy and well cared for and send them to their family. You may want to make some captions, like "Missing You," or "Hope You Are Having a Good Time."

141. Do Pet Parties.

Do you like animals? Some people treat their animals like their children. Some would love to have someone put on a nice birthday party for their pet. You could offer Pet Birthday or Adoption parties.

What is the potential market? There are millions of people who own pets in America. According to the *American Veterinary Medical Association*, 36.5% of American households own a dog. That is more than 43 million people. More than 33 million people own a cat. That is 30.4% of American households.

Have a theme for each party. One popular idea is to have the owners dress themselves and their pets according to the theme. Have prizes for the best costume sets.

Make sure you take pictures of the pets and owners with costumes or party hats on.

You may do well if you bring sets of costumed themed outfits for the pets to wear for photos. Get those for more than 50 percent off, after Halloween.

Consider making banners with the pet's names.

Consider little treat bags for each pet. That could include a party hat and some snacks and pet stickers.

Come up with some creative activities. Have a sing along. *Old MacDonald* is a good song to use. You may want to get a sound track of animals singing along and play that.

Make birthday treats for the pets and humans that go along with a theme. Get some dog or cat cookie cutters.

Bring helium balloons and DO NOT forget to sing *Happy Birthday*. Do a second verse in barks or meows.

For a Dog Party:

Play Fetch

Decorate some treats or dog bones with a ribbon. You can also use Frisbees or tennis balls.

Do an Agility Course

Set up easy to navigate obstacles the dogs, and maybe their owners, can run through or jump over. They could lead them through with a treat.

Play Bobbing for Biscuits

Have a nice large bowl in which you place doggie biscuits. Each dog gets a turn to get a biscuit.

Eating Contest

Buy or make special doggy treats and see who can finish eating them first. You can do this as a group or individually as a timed event.

Play Chase the Cat or Chase the Postman

Many dogs love this. It is probably best to use a wind-up cat. You could also have someone dress as a postman with a bag of mail and let the dogs chase them.

For a Cat Party:

Play Hide & Seek

Let the cat's sniff a catnip toy. Then hide it and see who finds it first.

Play Catch the Laser

This game is very popular with many cats. Get some

laser pointers and let the cats chase them.

You can do a variation of this with an obstacle course the owner must guide their cat through, prompting them to follow a laser pointer.

Play Catch the Mouse

Use real mice or wind-up toys.

Play Lick the Tuna Can

Most cats like licking out a tuna can. Make sure the edges are smooth, so they do not cut their tongue.

142. Spread Cremated Remains.

Spreading cremated remains is an important service you probably never considered, but one which you may be able to provide. This is one service, which is very important and has a lot of meaning to many people.

Cremated remains are considered sterile so there are no health risks associated with them.

Years ago, most people were buried after they died, hopefully not before. Now, more people are cremated. Those who are cremated often want their ashes sprinkled in a meaningful place. Some want them sprinkled where people who love them can come and remember them. Others want them sprinkled in the place where they were born, or where their family came from. Some want the sprinkled in some exotic place they loved or hoped to visit. Some want them spread at some special religious site.

I highly recommend people who plan to be cremated do not have their ashes sprinkled at their old homestead, unless that home has been, and will remain in the family for years to come. Future landowners may find it creepy knowing ashes are spread there. They also may not allow people to visit.

I recommend people spread at least some of the ashes at the grave of another loved one, such as a parent. That provides a family connection and place for people to visit. Then, if someone wants the ashes scattered some other place, I recommend they pick a place that is meaningful to them or their family, where they can visit. Some will still want them spread at some exotic or remote location.

You can offer the service of sprinkling ashes at graveyards or other areas, such as the ocean, a mountain, or some other special place. This service could be provided for the remains of a person or of a pet.

If you plan to scatter ashes in the ocean in the United States, the *Environmental Protection Agency* (EPA) prohibits scattering ashes on beaches or within three miles of shore. They also require you to report such distributions to the EPA within 30 days, with the point of departure, the name of the vessel and the latitude and longitude marker.

You may scatter cremated remains from the air, such as from a private airplane (you would be in big trouble if you tried to open the door on a commercial flight to do this), from a hot air balloon, or from a drone, as long as the remains, but not the container, are released.

You may have contacts in other geographic places who may be willing to assist you spreading the remains.

If you plan to ship the remains, in 2013 the United States passed regulations that cremated remains may only be mailed via the *United States Post Office* and not with *UPS* or *FedEx*. There are not any special requirements for sending cremated remains domestically in the mail, except they must be sent via Priority Mail. They advise labeling the package that it contains cremated remains, but that is not required. I have received remains through the United States Postal Service.

It is nice to say a simple prayer as you release the ashes. I recommend you take a digital picture of you, or someone else, releasing the ashes and of the place where they are released. It is also nice if you can provide GPS coordinates.

Your fee can vary greatly depending how far you travel. I recommend a minimum of $100 for a simple local distribution. Funeral Directors usually charge upwards of $500. If people desire to have their ashes scattered in an exotic or foreign place. Your fees should cover your costs to get to that destination.

If you travel overseas, or across a border to sprinkle ashes make sure you check travel regulations. Most airlines allow cremated remains to be transported in a carry on. They must not contain any metal or they will not be approved through security. Some airlines have very specific policies regarding transporting cremated remains. Some countries like the United Kingdom require them to be in a sealed container and accompanied by a Cremation Certificate. Most of those regulations apply to transporting entire cremated remains in urns or other containers. Small amounts, transported in luggage, and labeled may not be as much of a problem. When in doubt, check airline and country regulations.

Always be careful about any local regulations where you spread remains. In New York there are not any regulations forbidding the sprinkling of remains in public places, as long as it is not disruptive. Many buildings like the Empire State Building, do not allow you to sprinkle remains there. Those regulations were put in place to prevent people from sprinkling a whole urn of remains.

If you do not want to do this service and if you want to have your loved ones remains sprinkled in a special place, and cannot find anyone else to do it, please feel free to contact me. I offer such a service with a special prayer.

Some requests may seem extreme. There was a person who was a reenactor and loved history. He wanted his ashes shot out of a cannon at Washington's Crossing in Pennsylvania. His request was fulfilled. I have a cannon and can provide such a service if requested.

143. Provide Companionship.

This is a very important and meaningful service you may be able to provide. Most people need companionship. There are a variety of companionship services which people need and which you may be able to provide.

Some people need someone to visit them in their home. Some people need companions to go shopping with them or to go to social events or to travel with them. Some people can avoid going to assisted living places if they have some meaningful companionship.

A Companion is not a Caregiver. A Companion does not give any medical assistance, a Caregiver does. If you want to be a Caregiver, you will need professional training and most likely certification and licensing. A Companion only provides Companionship.

Even though you may escort someone to events, never use the term *escort* to identify yourself. Even though technically an *escort* is someone who escorts someone some place, the word escort has taken on a dark meaning, often involving elicit sexual relations.

144. Be a Live-in Companion.

Many people would rather have their loved ones remain in their homes than have them put into an assisted care facility. Some people can stay in their homes longer if they have a Live-In Companion or a Caregiver.

A Companion is someone who provides non-medical companionship services. A Live-In Companion lives with a person and helps with non-medical assistance, such as providing meals, as well as other non-medical assistance.

A Caregiver can provide some medical care. A Companion never administers any therapy of medications (including aspirin or vitamins).

Write & Publish

Have you ever wanted to write a book, and have it published? Or perhaps you are a good photographer or artist who would love to have your works published.

Did you know you can put together a book and get it professionally published with almost no cost to you? It is even possible you may have money from your first book in your bank account within 30 days.

To publish a book, you need: The Body of the Book, a Cover, an ISBN Number, and a Publisher.

The Body of the Book

The Body of the Book contains:

☐ **Title Page** – Includes the Title, Sub-Title and Author Name.

☐ **Publishing and Copyright Page** – Includes the publisher, ISBN number, copyright information, possible disclaimer, possible *All Rights Reserved* statement; and possibly a Dedication (that is optional and can also be added on an additional page).

☐ **Table of Contents** – Helpful but optional.

☐ **List of Illustrations** – Helpful but optional.

☐ **Introduction** – Optional. This is a good place to include any acknowledgements.

☐ **Main Body** – This is the main body of the book which includes the text and may include illustrations. It helps if at least every other page is numbered.

☐ **Index** – Optional but helpful for some non-fiction.

☐ **Bibliography** – Optional for fiction but recommended for non-fiction.

☐ **About the Author** – A one-page summary and possibly a picture.

A Cover

They say, *you cannot judge a book by its cover*, but most people do. Have someone help you may a good eye-catching cover for your book.

If you use either *Amazon* or *IngramSpark* publishing, they have templates you must follow for covers.

Both publishers give the choice of glossy or matte for covers. Most consumers prefer the glossy covers.

If you choose to make a hardcover book you can choose

to publish one with or without a dust jacket (that is a printed paper cover). If you get one with a dust jacket the actual hardcover may have the same cover image as the paper cover or it can be plain with just the title on the spine of the book. Most people like the hardcover printed with the same image as the dust jacket. It is popular to print hardcover books without dust jackets.

Your Cover needs a Front, Spine and Back:

☐ **The Front** – Includes the title of the book; perhaps a sub-title; an image; and author's name. It may also have a marketing phrase.

☐ **The Spine** – Includes the title of the book (not including the sub-title) and the author's last name.

☐ **The Back** – Includes the ISBN number; bar code; the price; whether the book is fiction or non-fiction; usually a catchy summary of the book; and sometimes a very brief biography of the author.

An ISBN Number

Every published book should have an ISBN (International Standard Book Number) number. If you use *CreateSpace* they will provide one at no cost, but that number will belong to them and you cannot republish it any place else.

You need a different ISBN number for every different version of a book. You need one if you do a print version and another for a digital version of the same book.

If you publish with *Ingram* you will need to buy your own ISBN. They will direct you to *Bowker*, who sells ISBN numbers. It is more cost effective to buy ISBN numbers in groups of 10 or 100.

A Publisher

You need someone to publish your book. There are a few different choices:

☐ **Traditional Publisher** - You can try to get your book published by a traditional publisher, but that is very difficult. If you secure such a deal, you will make pennies on the dollar for each book sold.

My first few books were published this way and I made about $0.60 for each $10 book sold.

The advantage of this is, they will market your book.

☐ **Agency or Small Publisher** - You can have a self-publishing agency or small publisher publish a book for you. That usually requires upfront money and you cover all printing cost and fees. You promote and sell these yourself, but you will make more money per book sold than with a traditional publisher.

☐ *Amazon or Ingram*. *Amazon* and *Ingram* offer an incredible twist on self-publishing. You write and submit the book and put together a final project. They publish the book and it ends up for sale online.

You may pay a small set-up fee and then pay for whatever copies you order. They pay you a percentage of online sales. You can also buy copies at their print cost and sell them yourself.

Amazon uses their *Kindle* subsidiary for self-publishing. You can publish paperback books or digital books with them. They do not do hardcover books.

Ingram, one of the world's largest publishers, offers self-publishing through *IngramSpark*. They publish paperback, hard cover, and digital books. They use higher quality paper than *Amazon*. They distribute books online and can offer digital versions through *Nook* at *Barnes & Noble*.

Unlike *Amazon*, *Ingram* has a catalog and distributes directly to schools, libraries, and publishers. With *Ingram* bookstores can buy your books at a discount and resell them. They have a higher set-up fee than *Amazon*, more stringent layout requirements, and you pay a fee if you want to be listed in their catalog.

Writing Your Book

To write a book you must determine what your book is going to be about and who is your target audience? The target audience is who you are writing it for.

Determine the size you want the book to be. I do that because I write my book and lay it out at the same time. You do not have to do that, but I like to know what the book is going to look like as I write it.

Both *Amazon* and *Ingram* have layout dimensions and templates available for both the Body of the book and the Cover. I set my page sizes and margins in *Word* and then write my book. That is so much better than the way I wrote my first few books. For those first books, I used an old manual typewriter.

The advantage of using a computer and a program like Word for writing your book is you can write out an outline and random thoughts as they come to you. Later you can cut and paste and rearrange and expand on them any way you like. It save a lot of trees.

If you are going to use illustrations in your book, they should be at least 300 dpi (dots per inch) and cannot be images someone else has a copyright on, unless you get permission to use those images.

After you finish writing the Main Body of your book, set it aside for a week or longer, then come back and read it. Correct the mistakes you find and make any other changes you think should be made.

Next, submit your book to at least two other people to read it. Ask them to make any corrections or suggestions. They need to be people who understand grammar, spelling, and are willing to be honest with you.

As you go back and make recommended corrections or changes, that may require you to make additional changes.

After you finish the first edit of your book, if it is non-fiction, determine if it needs an Index. Generating an Index is a tedious process but is often appreciated by many readers.

Determine if you want your book to be paperback or hardcover. According to *NPD BookScan*, during the first three quarters of 2018, 56% of all books sold were trade paperback, 27% were hardcover and 8% were the smaller mass market size paperback books.

If you want it to be paperback you can use either *Amazon* or *Ingram*. If you want it to be hardcover you will need to use *Ingram*.

Determine the Price for your book. First look at the production cost for the book. Then try to price it comparable to similar books on the market. Make the price high enough to offset a 30-55% reseller discount if you want bookstores to sell your book.

Next, make a good cover for your book.

After that, submit your book to the publisher.

If your book is approved, review a proof copy, then approve it for publishing.

Once approved for processing, buy some copies of your book, and begin to sell them. You will make more money if you order some of your own books, at your cost, and then resell them yourself than when the publisher sells them.

Next, you need to market your book. You may write a good book, but no one will know about it and buy it, unless they know about it. You should promote your book by writing some news releases and using social media.

The following are many ways you may be able to generate income by writing your own book and getting published.

145. Write a Fiction Book.

Some of the best-selling individual books of all time are fiction. If you write a good fiction book you may be able to generate some significant income.

Fiction is the category of books which consists of stories which people make up. It starts with an idea and is expanded upon by the writer's imagination.

In 1995, a 30-year-old divorced mother, living on state benefits, just one step away from homelessness wrote a novel on an old manual typewriter. She submitted it to twelve different publishers. They all rejected her manuscript, but she did not give up. It took two years for her book about a boy named Harry Potter to be published. Only 1,000 copies were printed, 500 of those went to libraries. The next year *Scholastic Inc.* paid $105,000 for the right to reprint her book. Joanne Rowling continued to write more books and each one became a best seller. The books were made into movies. The money kept coming in until she became a billionaire and was listed as the richest person in England.

There are many types of fiction books. Some are written for children, some for adults. They can be simple short stories, picture books, or long intricate novels. They can be based on historical events and people or they can take place in a totally made up magical world.

You will do best if you write about what interests you. Let your imagination guide you.

One of the best tools for writing today is the computer. You can write down your thoughts and outlines and keep rearranging them and adding to them until you have completed your book.

146. Write a Non-Fiction Book.

According to *NPD BookScan*, during the first three quarters of 2018, the largest selling category of books sold were Non-fiction. They accounted for about 52% of all books sold. The top three selling categories of books were: Adult Non-fiction with 43% of the market, followed by Juvenile Fiction with 22% and Adult Fiction with 20%.

Non-fiction books are those which are factual. They can be histories (though some of them seem more like fiction to me), biographies, how to books, philosophy, science, math, art, religion (lots of fiction there too), travel guides, cookbooks, manuals, and much more.

Most people do not realize they probably know enough, or have experienced enough, to write a book.

If you have done any research, then writing a book may be a great way for you to share the results of your research with others and generate some income at the same time.

All the books I published so far are non-fiction, but I have been working on a series of historical novels called *The New World Chronicles,* for quite a few years and hope to finish the first one soon and get it published.

147. Publish a Collection of Photographs.

Many people like books with photographs in them. If you like to take pictures you may want to consider publishing a book of your pictures. You can use old pictures you or others you know took, or you can take new pictures specifically for your book.

You cannot use any pictures which others copyrighted, or those of yours which have already been published in copyrighted works, unless you hold the copyright to them.

Your book could be pictures of people or places. You could think of a theme and go take pictures related to that. It could be of local sites or events. It could feature specific types of people. It could be of flora or fauna. It could be of wildlife or pets. There are so many possibilities.

You can take the pictures yourself or use the time-proven method of conducting a photo contest where people submit photos to be published in your book. Each entry you select for publication could receive a free copy of the book and an offer to buy additional books at a discounted rate. It is very likely many friends and relatives, of those who had their pictures published in your book, will purchase copies.

148. Do a Photo History Book.

Many people love photo history books. These are often called *coffee-table books*. If you like history and like to take pictures you may be able to put together one of these.

Some publishing companies specialize in photo books. Some focus on local or regional photo books. They are often looking for photographers and writers. I was approached by one of those companies to write a book for them. I like the work they did but decided to write my own.

I put together a local photo history book called, *Now and Then, Putnam County, New York*. That book contains pictures from all six towns in Putnam, County. It includes pictures of what places and buildings looked like more than 50 years ago, along with a picture of what they look like now. Many of the old pictures were from old postcards or archival photographs. Some of those older photographs were black and white, some were color. I took all the new pictures in color. I then published the book in color and received glowing reviews. You may want to look at a copy of that book to get an idea of what you can do in your area.

149. Publish a Collection of Artwork.

Many people like artwork. There are a number of ways you may be able to generate income publishing a book of art. You do not even have to be artistically inclined.

For many years some publishing companies held contests for art to be published in a coffee-table type book, similar to the photo contest idea mentioned for the photography book. Many charge an entry-fee to have the artwork considered for publication. Those selected are published in a book, which they offer at a reduced rate to those who submitted artwork. Most of those selected will buy more than one copy for family and friend. This is an easy way for someone to make money publishing a book with a built-in market.

You may want to use that model and you could do an art contest to collect art and publish a book. You could select a variety of themes for different books. It could be regional, environmental, or perhaps ethnic or cultural.

If you are artistically inclined, or if you know people who are, you may be able to gather enough artwork to publish an art book. Many people would love to see their artwork in a book.

You may want to visit some local art galleries, studios, school, or art shows to find artists whose work you like and who you may want to approach to include in your book.

Your book could be a collection of artwork with simple captions, or you could include more text with background about the artist and each piece of art featured.

If your art book is going to include color it is usually best to use a publisher such as *IngramSpark*. I also recommend publishing an art book as a hardcover book.

150. Do a Photo Book of People.

Many people love to see pictures of themselves. They would be ecstatic if they saw themselves or people they know in a book. This type of book can have a high appeal in a local market. This may not seem to be something which would generate much income, but it can.

Your book could feature close-ups of individuals or groups of people. It could focus on a theme. It could be a book of local people or could feature a much broader range of people.

Consider this scenario. If you put together a book with pictures including 500 people from your area and had only two pictures to a page, your book would be about 260 pages long (including title page, contents, and other ancillary pages). You could publish that as a hardcover book in 8" x 10" format with *IngramSpark*. If you priced them to sell at $29.95, it would cost you about $15 per book to buy them. If each person bought one copy, you would make about $7,500. That does not count the money you make from the sales generated by *IngramSpark* and their distributors. It is likely not all of the 500 people would buy a copy of the book, but it is likely some will buy two or three copies, or more, to give to friends and relatives. That would generate much more income for you. Now imagine if your book had pictures of 1,000 people.

151. Do a Photo Book of Animals.

People love books with pictures of animals. When we conducted a book sale for our fire department we had many books donated with pictures of animals. There were large coffee-table size books and very small pocket-sized books. I noticed those books sold very fast.

A picture book of animals could feature almost any kind of animal and could be geared to appeal to almost any age group.

You can take pictures of animals yourself, or you can use the time-proven method of conducting a photo contest. People submit photos of animals to be published in your book. Each entry you select for publication gets a free copy of the book and an offer to buy additional books at a discounted rate. Many friends and relatives will purchase copies.

152. Publish a Book of Poetry.

Do you like poetry? If you do, you may want to consider publishing a book of poetry.

You can either write and publish your own poetry or conduct a poetry contest and publish the poems people submit. Many people would love to see their poetry published. You provide a copy of the book to people who submit poems, either free for a significant discount and allow them to buy additional copies. Many friends and relatives will purchase copies.

Another idea is to put together a selection of classic poems from the public domain.

153. Publish a Family History.

Many people love to learn more about their family history and are willing to buy family history books.

Many people buy books about their surname, even if they are not well written. Some publishers specialize in writing very generic books about popular surnames. They often include a list or famous people with that surname and include a current directory listing the name and address of people with that surname. I personally consider those a waste of money, but people still buy them.

Well researched family history books are often self-printed in very limited runs because they appeal to a limited market. They often sell for a lot of money. It is not unusual for them to sell for $100 or much more.

The market for such books are generally to people who are either mentioned in the books, or who have a known or presumed ancestor included in the book. These books especially appeal to libraries and historic sites in localities where those with the family named in the book live.

Some genealogy programs such as *Family Tree Maker* have a feature which enables you to input family data and then print a family history book. Some people print those books using a personal computer and printer. They put them in a notebook and offer them for sale. It is much more cost effective for you, and much more attractive to buyers, if you print such a project using *CreateSpace* or *IngramSpark*. You will also have a much broader market.

The more photographs and images of people and places you include, the more desirable your book will be.

This is a project which can generate income for you and become a treasured item to many people.

154. Publish a Book of Recipes.

Recipe books have been popular for many years. When we conducted a book sale for our fire department we had more cookbooks donated and sold than we did of any other type of non-fiction book.

Recipe books have been put together and used as fund raisers for many organizations, especially by Ladies Auxiliary Groups over the years.

You can put together a book of your own recipes or you

could do a recipe contest. The people whose recipes you use receive a copy of the book and an opportunity to buy additional copies at a reduced price. Many friends and relatives will purchase copies.

155. Update or Republish & Sell Old Books.

If you like old books you may be able to make money republishing or updating old books in the *Public Domain*.

Public Domain refers to books without a copyright, or ones whose copyright has expired. Anyone can publish such works and are not required to pay royalties to anyone.

If you want to republish a work in the public domain, make sure the version of the text you use, along with any illustrations, are not newer revisions which may have been copyrighted by someone.

Expanded or Illustrated

You may want to add your own introduction, introductions to chapters, illustrations, or add notes to explain passages. You could also add discussion sections at the end of each chapter. That will make your work more unique. You then copyright your work. That does not protect the public domain text you use, but it does copyright everything else.

Update Language

You could update an old work, which uses old style archaic language, such as thee, thou and ye, with contemporary language.

Paraphrase

To paraphrase a book means to change the words so they maintain the original intent yet are written in way a modern reader would better understand.

Abridge

To abridge a book means to shorten it and make it more concise.

Your abridgement could be geared to younger readers.

156. Be a News Correspondent.

If you want to work for a large newspaper it helps to have a degree in journalism and years of experience. However, there are many local daily and weekly papers which desperately need writers.

Years ago, some reporters worked as *stringers*. That is how I started. A stringer was basically a sub-contractor who wrote stories for the newspaper. When their stories were published they would cut out their stories and glue or tape them together column after column as a long string of paper, and they were paid by the inch, hence the name stringers. Most papers paid a bonus if a story appeared on the front page of a section. Most also paid bonuses if photographs you took were used.

Many newspapers still use stringers, though the way they are paid varies. Most newspapers are always looking for good stringers but there is a lot of competition.

If you want to be a new reporter, study your local weekly newspaper. See how the articles are written. Then attend an event and write a story and immediately send it to the paper. They may use that story and then want more.

I started writing as a reporter that for the *Times of Ti* out of Ticonderoga, New York. I went to whatever events I could, interviewed participants and spectators, took pictures, wrote a story, and submitted it for publication. The more I wrote the better my stories became.

I learned the importance of writing a story that explains an event the way a reader would like to understand it. If there was any controversy I always made sure I found both sides and included that in my articles.

An editor of a larger daily newspaper called *The Glens Falls Post Star* saw my stories and photos. He contacted me and asked me to write for his paper and to take pictures. I quickly ended up with stories and pictures on the front page. That earned me more money.

Many of my stories and pictures went out across the *AP (Associated Press)* and appeared in other papers. As a result of that, I won the *First Place Associated Press Writing Award*.

I was then contacted by the *United Press International (UPI)* and became a journalist for them.

I do not have a degree in journalism but was paid to write for newspapers. When I started to write for the weekly paper I never expected I would eventually be writing stories distributed around the country and would receive a national award beating out thousands of people with journalism degrees. Maybe you can do the same?

Entertainment Related

You may think you do not have talent which can generate additional income. You may be surprised. Some of these methods in this category do not need any talent. In fact, there are many people in the entertainment industry who have very little talent. What they have is personality or connections.

During economic hard times many people do not cut down on their entertainment expenses, therefore there are almost always opportunities in that category for you to generate some income.

157. Do Commercials.

You be able to generate income by being part of a commercial. There are both national and local companies who always need people to be in the commercials they make.

When I as a child, many commercials were filmed live. Sometimes I appeared in commercials during some of the television programs my father worked on.

Companies who make commercials need ordinary people. My mother once was in a commercial for Gravy Train Dog Food.

One of my best friend's took his son to try out for a commercial. He was selected. As a result of that commercial he ended up having a regular role in a weekly sitcom.

I have a friend who was paid $25,000 to be in a Super Bowl commercial. He said it only took three hours to film.

Watch out for agencies. Many of them charge fees and have you sign contracts you will later regret. Be careful what you sign. Anyone who provides a service to get you in a commercial should only be paid if you are paid. Look online for guidelines about negotiating contracts.

158. Be a Movie Extra.

Over the years, I worked on a number of film projects. Many of them hire extras for a day, a week or longer. The standard rate, as I write this, is $150 a day, plus food and sometimes lodging. This is a good way to get free meals and earn some money at the same time.

If you put together a few outfits that can help you get more work. Smaller productions do not have much of a costume budget and are always looking for people with good outfits. I have a friend Brian who learns all he can about a film shoot and goes with a few outfits that might be appropriate. That had secured him some extra work.

Bigger productions usually provide costumes but often like people who have their own historically accurate costumes. I have don work for ones like that.

Do not worry if you are not the most beautiful or handsome person or that you are out of shape or are missing a bunch of teeth. You may have a much better chance getting hired than the Miss America runner-up.

If you are too self-conscious about how you look, you may want to consider being an extra for a zombie movie. They are some of the least picky in their casting.

Have someone take good pictures of you in costume for a portfolio. Make sure they are good pictures that highlight what is key about you and show a variety of expressions.

Some suggested costumes which can be helpful, though not necessary, if you want to be ready to be a movie extra:

Dress Clothing

Make sure you have both business and formal attire. Woman should have a few different outfits. Some basic mix and match skirt, blouse and slack combinations can give you multiple looks.

Men can use different ties to change their look. I have a few friends who gets work because they brings a few changes of clothing to the filming. That lets them be used multiple times in multiple scenes.

In a few film projects I worked on, we used the same people and just had them swap hats or outer clothing.

Historical Outfits

This is a good way to open many doors. Looking accurate is very helpful.

159. Make Audio Books.

Many people like to listen to books instead of reading them. Many listen to them on portable devices or in their car. If you have a clear voice you may be able to start making some audio books to resell at no cost to you.

First, pick a book, which is in the public domain. That means there is either no copyright or the copyright expired. Many older books fall into that category. That includes books by Charles Dickens, William Shakespeare, Greek Classics, and thousands more.

Hook up a good microphone to your computer and start your recording. Save your book in a mpg or similar format, which can be used on a portable audio device, computer, or phone. It is best to pause between chapters, so each chapter becomes an individual file,

Read clearly and dramatically. If you can use different voices for different characters that is a plus but not necessary. If you can play some non-copyrighted music in the background during transitions, that is even better.

If you do this well, you will get followers who will want other books you read. If you are really good, a publisher may contact you and hire you to record books for them.

You can also offer a CD Version of your audio book, though there is much less demand for that. You can do that by copying your files to some re-writable CD's.

160. Be a Model.

You may be able to generate some income doing some modeling. Perhaps you have never considered being a model. Perhaps it seems intimidating.

You do not need to be a super model to be a model. Too many people think of international modeling and forget there may be a need for model in your own area for local manufacturers, companies, or stores.

There is always a need for models of all ages, shapes, sizes, and ethnicities. You can even be a model for a specific body part. I have a relative who was a hand model.

It is good to put together personal portfolio of pictures. You can hire a professional photographer to do that or may be able to find a friend to do it, or you may be able to do it yourself. The cameras on many smart phones have a higher resolution than the old 35mm film cameras and can take nice photos.

Watch out for portfolio scams who promise to get you modeling jobs but charge hundreds to take your pictures.

There are some model websites where you can make your photos and services available.

Be very careful which jobs you accept. Be safe. Never go alone. Make sure the people or company requesting you are reputable.

161. Be a D.J.

Do you like music? D.J.s, also known as *Disc Jockeys*, technically provide a mix of music at events. Some do more than just play music. Some provide coordinated light shows and serve as an announcer for an event. You may be able to earn some money as a D.J.

This can be done for local parties, weddings, Bar Mitzvas, Pet Parties, store openings, anniversaries, political rallies, concerts, craft shows, retirement homes (these often need people) or other events.

You can do this with a simple sound system and provide background music and announcements. Or you can also do this in a very advanced way adding a light show, turntables and more.

Twice a year there is a great Military Collectable Show in Patterson, New York sponsored by my friends Brian and Jennie Benedict from *The Duffle Bag*. Often a D.J. comes with a basic sound system, microphone and selection or music geared to military eras, such as World War II.

To be a D.J. all you need is a sound system (that can be a combination amplifier, digital music player and speaker) a microphone and selection of tunes.

Try to get a variety of playlists for different target audiences. You can then advertise the genres you have.

There are some legal considerations to be a D.J. You must only play music you own, you may not copy someone else's music to use. There are royalties, which have to paid when someone else' music is played in front of other group of people. Paying those royalties is not the D.J.'s responsibility. That is the venue's responsibility.

162. Enter a Talent Show.

Many contemporary entertainers have made it big because they entered a talent show. There are small local talent shows you may be able to participate in and some big ones like *American Idol, So You Think You Can Dance* or *America's Got Talent*.

To get on those shows it helps if you have some talent, but it helps even more if you have a personal touching story. You may have a more touching story than you realize. Think of personal, economic, social, or family struggles you or your family are facing or came through.

For example, maybe one of your grandparents loved music in the old country and came to America and laid aside their dreams of becoming a professional musician so they could provide for your father or mother. Then they passed that love for music on to your father or mother who wanted to pursue that musical career, but life happened, and they were unable to follow that dream. Now it is finally your chance and you want to fulfill that dream before your grandparents die. They love stories like that.

Or maybe you had a tough time in school because you were ADHD, overweight, or were bullied. To help provide you a loving friend your parents got a dog for you. You really bonded with that dog. Your dog helped you get through some hard times. You did not feel comfortable singing around other people but when you sang with your dog you felt special because your dog would lay close to you and make you feel loved. Your dog is getting old now and has given you the confidence to enter the talent show. You want to win for your loving pet and all those other people whose pets have helped them through hard times.

Believe it or not, a touching back story like those might get you through to audition before the judges.

If you do not have a touching story you may be able to get through if you are extreme or outlandish. Just one appearance on an episode might change your life.

Many local talent shows have fees to offset their expenses. It does not cost anything to enter *American Idol* or *America's Got Talent*. You just sign up and show up for your audition. You may also submit a video audition.

American Idol is only for singers. You must be a singer between the ages of 15 and 28.

So You Think You Can Dance is for individual or group dancers. You must be able to dance a wide variety of styles.

For *America's Got Talent* you can be any age and have almost any conceivable talent from singing, playing an instrument, dancing, magic, acrobatics, daredevil stunts, or doing a comedy routine. Your talent can even be macabre or ridiculous.

You may even get on one of those shows because of what you wear. I appeared on three seasons of *America's Got Talent* because I wore Revolutionary War uniforms.

If you audition for either a local on national talent program, practice what you are going to do and dress for the part. You must understand they will begin to judge you the moment they lay eyes on you. They will look at what you wear, how you walk, what you say and then what you do. Do it well and with all your heart.

163. Provide a Costumed-Themed Service.

Put together a unique outfit and offer a service delivering birthday greetings or other special messages in your outfit. You can sing them, recite them, or read them. You can also offer your services for events, birthday parties or trade shows. Some people love to have costumed characters present.

You can list this service on *Facebook* or *Craigslist* at no cost to you.

You cannot legally promote yourself and charge for your services as a licensed character. For example, you can advertise yourself as a princess but not as *Snow White*.

Men, if you are doing a princess character you should shave your beard.

Make your own outfits or get ones for 25-90% off after Halloween. Over the years, I picked up *Star Trek* uniforms after Halloween for at least 75% off. I can outfit a small crew. My oldest son likes *Star Trek*. We wore *Star Trek* uniforms to his Wedding Rehearsal.

Look at Costume or CosPlay *(Costume Play)* sites for ideas for costumes.

Some Possible Costumes to Consider:
Cowboy or Cowgirl
Wear a cowboy hat, boots, jeans and bandana.

Fantasy or Fairy Tale Character
Fairies, Elves and Hobbits are popular,

Sci-Fi
This is a broad category. You could dress up as anything from *Star Wars, Star Trek*, Super Heroes, Aliens, Vampires or Godzilla.

Historical Figures
This provides a broad range of characters, from Cave Person, Roman, Hun, Viking, Knight, Musketeer, Pilgrim, Revolutionary War Soldier and Roaring Twenties, to specific historical characters.

You do not have to be 100% authentic looking to do this but if you are, you will probably get better business.

If you want to dress as a Revolutionary War soldier you may want to get a copy of my book, *You Can Make a Revolutionary War Regimental Coat*.

Santa's Helper
Many people love to have Santa Claus attend their holiday events but due to his busy schedule he is not available. Perhaps you could dress as one his helpers? He does not mind people dressing to look like him, as long as they are nice and jolly. Some people naturally look the part. You could even go as one of his Elfs.

Just a small technical point. Some of us in the CosPlay/Sci-Fi world make a distinction between an Elf and an Elve. An Elf works for Santa, fix shoes or makes cookies in trees. An Elve usually lives in the woods and appears in places like *Middle Earth* and *Narnia*. They often get their cookies from the Elfs.

Storybook Characters
There are many storybook characters. Some popular ones are princesses, princes, pirates, wizards, and fairy godmothers. To be unique you could add a comedic twist to your character.

Animals

Everyone loves cute cuddly characters. Just be careful you DO NOT come across scary. As a child, I was scared by a six foot tall Easter Bunny.

Clowns

For some reason clowns are very popular. Make sure you look funny, not scary, or creepy.

Ninja

I caution against this one unless you have some martial arts experience. Many children are taking martial arts today and may test their skills on you.

164. Sing or Play an Instrument.

Singing or playing an instrument is a time-tested way to generate income.

Depending on where you live, you may not really need to have much talent to do this. Many popular recording artists are not very good musicians. Some of them cannot play an instrument and can barely carry a tune, but they make up for it with personality and presentation.

A lot of being a successful professional musician is marketing and keeping active. As long as you can play or sing a few songs, there will be open doors. The better you are at presenting yourself, the more people will pay you.

You do not even need back up instrumentalists. Many musicians bring pre-recorded back-up music which them to play as they perform. In some venues, it is not unusual for professional musicians do lip-synching to recorded music. That means their pre-recorded background music also has their voice on the track. They mouth the words or sing along with their microphone off. If you choose to lip-synch, make sure you do it very well or humorously bad.

If you want to play an instrument but have tried and none seem to work for you, let me recommend the *Q-Chord* by Suzuki. It is an electronic *Autoharp*. If you have any sense of rhythm you can play a beautiful tune on the

Q-Chord or *Autoharp* in just a few minutes.

The *Autoharp* is the first instrument I played. It is a 36 stringed instrument with a beautiful sound. Johnny Cash's mother-in-law, *Mabelle Carter* played one. The *Rolling Stones* also used one. It had a series of chord bars with felt pads which mute strings when depressed, so only the right strings for the chord you depressed played as you strum it. I loved playing the *Autoharp,* but it had 36 strings which need to be tuned. They are quite expensive to replace.

There is an electronic version of the Autoharp. I first saw one when I was visiting my friend *Clarence Canary*. I met Clarence when I was chaplain at *Frontier Town*. He told me he ran away from home when he was 12 years old and joined *Buffalo Bills Wild West Circus*. He was an expert shot and even in his 80's he could shoot a quarter from across a rodeo arena with a six shooter in his hand and his back turned to the target, using a mirror to see. Clarence also learned to become an excellent leather worker. He made many of the harnesses used on the elephants and other animals in the *Ringling Brothers, Barnum & Bailey Circus* and by *Disney*.

One day, while I was visiting Clarence, a UPS Truck arrived and delivered a box. That made him as excited as a young boy in a candy shop. It contained an *Omnichord*.

The *Omnichord* was the first electronic version of the *Autoharp*. He showed it to me and said he always wanted to learn to play an instrument. He told me, "I better learn now because I do not have much time left."

In just a few minutes, this man with no musical background whatsoever, was playing a beautiful tune.

A few years after that, I bought a *Q-Chord*, the successor to the *Omnichord*. I often take it to conferences with me and let people, who have never played an instrument, play it. Immediately they are playing a beautiful song and people sing along with them.

It may be worth the investment for you to get a Q-Chord if you want to play an instrument quickly and earn additional income. You can get them on *eBay* for around $200-300.

Here is some advice for making money singing or playing an instrument:

Record and Post Some Songs on YouTube.

Record some songs and post them on *YouTube*. This is a good starting place. That helps people become familiar with you. It lets you see if people really like you or if your relatives, who said you sing and play nice, did that because they love you or are tone deaf.

NEVER record and sell music someone else has the copyright to, without written permission.

Set Up a PayPal Account

By setting up a free *PayPal* account, you will be able to receive payments for music you sell.

Record and Sell Some Songs On-line

Unless you recorded and sold a lot of music, *iTunes* probably will not sell your music. Record some songs and upload them to online sites like *Bandcamp*. They currently give you 85% of your sales.

You can use a service like *TuneCore*. They charge more but may get a broader distribution for your music.

NEVER record and sell any music someone else has the copyright to, without written permission.

Record Your Own CDs

Many people moved away from CDs a long time ago but if you want to make some CDs to market to an older generation, you can make some on your computer.

Record songs on your computer. Then transfer them to a CD with your computer's writeable CD/DVD drive. Some printers let you design graphic images for the CDs themselves, which you can print right onto certain CDs. You can put them in clear plastic CD holders, or make inserts and put them in CD Jewel Cases. This method is the poor man's way to produce CDs.

Make a Sign to Use When You Perform

Here is a VERY IMPORTANT piece of advice. Make a sign to set out when you perform. This sign lets people know who you are. Make it look good.

Your sign should include two things: the name of your act and a QR Code. A QR code is a special black and white image, which takes people to a specific website if they scan it with their phone or tablet.

Look online for a site that lets you generate a free QR Code. The QR Code generator will create a free JPG image of a specific QR Code for that specific webpage. You save that image and put it on your sign.

Always set out your sign when you perform. If people like you they can scan your QR Code on their smartphone or tablet and it will immediately take them to the webpage where they can buy your songs. They do not have to type in anything. They can click and buy your music. All of that is done without you needing to spend money on CDs, nor having to carry and inventory or man a music table.

Put Together a Promotional Package

Include a one-sheet promo piece. Include a page of places you performed, which will recommend you. Include the styles of music you perform and type of events you do. Include a link to where they can download a few songs or include a DVD demo.

Play for Open Mike & Local Competitions

Open Mike Nights and Local Competitions are good places to get practice and exposure before a live audience. The level of talent at Open Mike places is usually low and the audiences are usually appreciative of any real talent. This can help you polish your act.

They may let you sell some CDs (if senior citizens are present). You can pass out promo pieces with a link to where they can download your songs online. Be sure to set out your sign with your QR Code on it.

Play for Restaurants

Some eating establishments hire live entertainment. Some just want instrumentals for background music. Some want a full-blown stage show.

Play for Weddings

Many people want live music at their wedding. They usually want you to do cover songs. You may want to throw in a couple of originals between the covers.

Play for Parties

There is a big market of people looking for live entertainment for parties. They usually want cover songs, but you can throw in some originals.

Play for Funerals

People will hire singers to play the organ or piano and to sing at some funerals.

If you can play *Amazing Grace* and perhaps, *Going Home*, on the bagpipes or *Q-Chord* you will probably be able to keep busy. I often sing *Amazing Grace* acapella (without instrumentation).

Play for Local Events

Fairs and other community events often look for live music. Some pay and some have competitions with prize money. Make sure you display your sign.

Play on the Street

Some towns allow street performers to play in public and collect donations. Some place require a permit.

Set out an open music case, a hat, or other container to receive donations. It is a good idea to *sweeten the pot*. That means you put in some $5, $10 or $20 bills in the collection box for people to see. That will make some people consider giving more than just $1.

Have your sign prominently displayed. Some people who like you will use the QR Code, go to your site and download some or your songs.

Record Commercial Jingles

Most products use a musical jingle. Local advertisers need people to sing or play for their local advertising.

165. Write Music.

If you love music why not try writing some. Every songwriter started with a first song.

You may be able to make a significant amount of money writing songs.

Some people are paid to write the words to songs, some are paid to write the musical arrangement and others are paid to play the song. Some do all three, some only do one of those tasks. All of them are paid every time a song is performed or played on the radio.

Maybe you could write simple songs, love songs, choruses, ballads, or jingles for local businesses.

I remember hearing Barry Manilow say he started out in the music business writing jingles. Some of his jingles became very successful such as: *Like a good neighbor State Farm is there*; *I am stuck on Band-aid brand cause Band-aid's stuck on me;* and the iconic, *You deserve a break today, so get up and get away to McDonalds*.

Miscellaneous Ways

The following are a few Miscellaneous Ways you may be able to use to generate some additional income.

166. Be a Product Tester.

A number of manufacturers are always looking for product testers. That can be tasting food, trying health products, or testing equipment.

A few classmates and I were paid for participating in a variety of these when I was in college.

One company had us come in and taste a product. We

then gave our opinion of both the packaging and the product itself.

Another company had us use their health care product. We then met with a representative from the company and gave them our opinion. It was easy money.

You can find many opportunities for these online. Valid opportunities never charge anything. They pay you to participate you do not pay them.

167. Participate in Research Studies.

Many universities pay people to participate in research studies. Some are as simple as filling out a survey, answering questions or attempting some task.

As I was writing this section, *New York University* had 59 different studies where they were willing to pay people to participate. The majority of those studies are one to two hours long. Some are for two days. They offer from $10-25 per hour.

You can maximize your time by participating in multiple studies simultaneous. Perhaps you can do one study in the morning and one in the afternoon. You may line up studies with different universities in the same area for different times on the same day. Some people earn $100 or more a day doing this.

168. Enter Contests & Sweepstakes.

Many places and companies offer contests and sweepstakes. They are often provided as a means to attract more customers. Entering contests is one way you may be able to generate income.

Some contests involve skills and if you have the skills you may be able to win. Some contests are strictly chance with no guarantees.

Publishers Clearing House offers some contests with some life-changing prizes. You do not have to purchase anything to enter, though they hope you do.

If it does not cost you to enter a contest, then my feeling is why not try?

Be careful if someone contacts you and says you won a sweepstakes you never entered. There are many scams which use that approach to get personal information from you.

Extreme Ways to Generate Income

Though SOME people may consider some of the other methods of generating income in this book as extreme, MOST people would probably consider ALL the following methods extreme.

Though these methods are extreme, they have been used successfully by some people to generate income. Perhaps one of them will work for you.

169. Sell Your Hair.

If you have good healthy, undyed hair, are not a smoker and can part with at least 10 inches of hair, there is a good possibility you can sell your hair.

Some people donate their hair to help others but maybe you are in a situation where you or your family needs additional income. There is nothing wrong with selling your hair to help your family.

Depending on the quality of your hair you can earn from $100-$4,000.

170. Sell Your Plasma.

You can donate or sell plasma up to twice a week. It is a lot like giving blood except they do not take the red blood cells. They return those back into your system. That is why it takes longer than giving blood.

The first visit can take two to three hours. Return visits

average 90 minutes. The current rate they pay for your plasma, per session is $50-150.

You cannot donate plasma if you use cocaine, heroin or other drugs. You also cannot donate plasma if you had a tattoo in the past 12 months.

If you lived in the United Kingdom during certain periods, you are restricted from giving plasma.

CSL Plasma [CSLPlasma.com] is one place to make contacts to donate or sell your plasma. They pay up to $300 per month. They even have a rewards program for frequent donors.

171. Participate in Clinical Trials.

There are many scientific studies looking for human guinea pigs. They will pay you to participate in a variety of studies. You will earn money and help advance some field of study and maybe help save lives. Those studies usually pay $2,000-$6,000.

The studies with more risk pay more to compensate for the increased risk, pain, and possible mutations, which you may experience. Make sure your read the small print.

You can find a listing of some of the safer current clinical trials at *ClinicalTrials.gov*. If you are more of a risk-taker you can contact Dr. Frankenstein or Dr. Moureau directly.

172. Make "Will Work for Food Sign."

People make money holding, "Will Work for Food" signs. I have spoken with some and discovered they had no intention of accepting any work offered to them. They found what they consider to be an easy way to make money, playing on people's sympathy.

This method may work well for you, if you really intend to work. Consider making a sign from an old cardboard box. On the sign write the words, *Will Work for Food*.

The key to doing this successfully is you must look like

you will work and not look like you will use the money for drugs or alcohol. Wear work clothes and perhaps a tool belt with some tools. It is probably best you do not hold an axe or chainsaw, even though they can be helpful tools.

DO NOT look destitute. Be sure to smile.

You may want to specify on the sign what type of work you are willing to do. Your sign could say, *Yard Work* or *Will Do Dirty Jobs*.

If your sign says *Computer Work* or *Tax Preparation*, be sure to wear a suit and have a briefcase. If your sign says *Will Cook*, wear a chef's hat and apron.

You may consider writing, *Need Someone to Listen to You? Pay Me and I Will Listen to You.*

173. Sell Your Breast Milk.

This method is sure to be considered extreme by many. But if you are a woman, and able to lactate, once of the most lucrative things you may be able to do is to produce and sell your breast milk. Some women in the United States earn in excess of $50,000 to $150,000 per year, selling their milk.

Here are Some Important Things to Consider:

You Do Not Have to Have a Baby to Produce Milk.

If you would like to sell breast milk pregnancy is the most common way to induce lactation, but there are other ways such as hypnosis and hormones which can help start lactation without being pregnant.

Mother's Milk is Healthy.

Scientific studies show mother's milk is the healthiest food for newborns and infants. It gains more nutritional value the longer a woman nurses.

Because of its nutritional value some doctors recommend mother's milk for other patients and creates a broader market.

According to a study conducted by *ABC News*, the average mother in America nurses their child for 6 months to one year. *The World Health Organization* (WHO), recommends nursing a child for a minimum of two years to as long as five to six years.

Some mothers are unable to produce milk, or choose not to personally nurse their children, yet want their children to have breast milk because of its nutritional value. That creates a market for breast milk.

How Much Milk Can You Produce?

Most women naturally produce enough milk to feed the children they birth, whether they have one child or triplets.

The average baby needs 25 to 35 ounces of milk a day. A woman nursing triplets will produce 75 to 105 ounces a day.

According to studies, the average woman who extracts their milk by pumping will produce an average of 2 to 3 liters every 24 hours, depending on the frequency and length of each milking. That equals 67 to 101 ounces. Some produce a lot more.

Who Can Sell Breast Milk?

If you are a healthy woman, who does not smoke or use drugs, you may be able to sell your breast milk. If you eat organic foods, your milk will be in greater demand.

Some women sell their milk for completely altruistic reasons, seeking to help those who need their milk. Some sell their milk for the lucrative financial compensation.

There are numerous online sites and classified ads dedicated to selling breast milk.

Producing & Extracting Your Milk.

To sell breast milk, you can extract the milk manually, but most do it with a breast pump.

According to some websites, where woman sell their

breast milk, many women nursing one child extract extra milk by pumping. That pumping often doubles or triples their production. That provides a significant amount to sell. Those who do that usually pump for an additional 10 to 20 minutes each time, 30 to 60 minutes before or after nursing their child.

Those who strictly pump their milk to resell must do so at least 6 to 7 times per day to maintain production. Many do it 8 times a day. That is once every 2.5 to 3 hours. They usually pump 10 to 15 minutes each time.

It is not the strength of the suction on the pump, but the length of the milking which produces more milk. To increase production, it is recommended you pump an additional 5 minutes after all the milk is extracted. That sends a signal to your body you need to produce more milk and your body responds.

How Much Does Breast Milk Sell For?

If you want to sell breast milk, most places want a minimum of 100 ounces at a time. Many participants freeze their milk, so they have a larger quantity to sell.

The price for breast milk will change. The current rate for frozen breast milk averages $1-$2 per ounce. Fresh local breast milk sells for $4-$5 per ounce. It can sell for more depending on your location. The prices are much higher in countries like England where more than $7 per ounce is common.

If you want to figure how much money you can make per hour of milking, consider the following:

☐ Most women can produce 67 to 101 ounces per day.

☐ If you pump for 15 minutes, 8 times a day, you will be pumping for a total of 2 hours a day.

☐ If you sell your milk for the minimum $1 per ounce, you could earn $67 to $101 per day, which is $33.50 to $50.50 per hour of actual milking. That can result in an income of $24,455 to $36,865 per year.

☐ If you sell your milk for $2 per ounce, you could

earn $134 to $202 per day, which is $67-101 per hour of actual milking). That can result in an income of $48,910 to $73,730 per year.

☐ You can multiply those figures if you sell your fresh breast milk for $4 to $5 per ounce.

How Long Can You Produce Milk to Sell?

Would you be surprised if I told you, you can produce and sell your milk for 20 years? You can even do it longer. As long as you stay healthy and keep extracting milk, your body will keep producing.

There is an old occupation known as *Nurse Maid* or *Wet Nurse*. Those are lactating woman, who nurse other people's children. In 1831, Judith Waterford, a Nurse Maid in England was still producing two quarts of milk (64 ounces) a day on her 81st birthday.

174. Sell Your Bone Marrow.

Bone Marrow is used to help treat some very serious life-threatening diseases such as *leukemia*. If you are in good health, you can register as a donor.

Though some believe this will change soon, the United States Government passed a law you may only sell your bone marrow if you live in one of the nine states covered by the *Ninth District Court*. That includes Alaska, Arizona, California, Hawaii, Idaho, Nevada, Oregon, Montana and Washington. You must do it through *MoreMarrowDonors.org*.

The process is quite painful and requires hospital visits. The compensation is $3,000 in the form of scholarships, housing allowances or donations to your favorite charity. The greatest need for donors is from the African American Community.

175. Lease Body Space.

Some companies pay people to wear a temporary or permanent tattoo, with their logo, on a visible body part.

One woman was paid $10,000 from *Golden Palace* to have the company's logo tattooed on her forehead.

LeaseYourBody.com is a website that provides various opportunities where you can get paid to wear a tattoo. You must agree to wear the tattoo, and keep it exposed for a certain amount of time.

Think very carefully before you do this. If you later choose to remove the tattoo, that is a painful and expensive proposition.

176. Host the Flu.

The *Center for Disease Control* will pay you $3,000 to be part of a study where they give you the flu. They say this helps them develop better vaccines. You must sign a disclaimer saying you understand there are serious possible side effects, including death.

177. Get Paid to Stay in Bed 70 Days.

The *National Aeronautics and Space Administration* (NASA) is a United States governmental agency, which conducts ongoing studies about the effects of weightlessness. They will pay you to stay in bed for 70 days as part of one of those studies. As of September 2018, NASA was paying participants $15,600.

One of the NASA scientists, speaking about the program, said the opportunity to participate in this program exists because many people cannot mentally handle 70 days of staying in bed.

You may also be able to participate in one of their other, more classified studies.

178. Other Ways to Generate Income.

I am sure there are many other ways to generate income you will discover if you do an internet search. Times are always changing and there are always new ways to generate income.

Important Considerations

Some methods for generating additional income can produce a significant amount of money. That may make you want to make some changes in your life. Some changes can be good, some can be bad. I strongly recommend you get good advice before you make any significant changes in your life.

As you seek advice, remember, not all advice is good. Find someone you trust, who has experience in life, who will tell you what you need to know, not what you want to hear.

Be willing to make necessary changes to help make life better for you and those around you.

Here is one very serious warning, it is okay to want more than you need but beware of the love of money, it will destroy you.

Though many of the methods for generating additional income will not require you to make significant changes to your life, the following are important items you must consider before undertaking some of these methods of generating income.

Evaluate and Make a Plan

The first and most important thing you need to do is to evaluate your current situation, get good advice, and then develop a plan. If you are married make sure you include your spouse in this process.

You Need to Answer the Following Questions:

1. What is your current source of income?
2. What is you total regular income?
3. What are your current expenses?

4. Can you reduce expenses?
5. Does your current employment allow you to meet your basic needs and wants?
6. Is there a set amount of money you are trying to generate?
7. Is that a one-time amount, or an amount you would like to see come in on a regular basis?
8. Is your current employment personally fulfilling?
9. Is there something you can do to make your current employment more fulfilling?
10. If additional income is needed is there a way to earn additional income from your current employment, such as working additional hours, an additional day, or an additional shift?
11. If the income from your current employment does not allow you to generate enough income to meet your needs and wants, where you currently live, does your employer have opportunities in places with a lower cost of living than where you live now?
12. What are your current responsibilities (including job, family, and other)?
13. How much time do you have available to commit to generating additional income, which will not conflict with your current responsibilities?
14. What method(s) interest you? Select a few.
15. What methods could you pursue right now?
16. What are the pros and cons of pursuing each method?
17. Do you need any tools or supplies?
18. Do you need start-up money?
20. Do you need to acquire or enhance any of your skill sets?
21. Which method(s) will you pursue?

Know Your Local Laws

Some people have found themselves in serious trouble while they sought to generate additional income because they did not know the law or disregarded it. Ignorance of the law is not an excuse. You will be held accountable if you do not follow the law.

It is very important you know your local laws. Many municipalities have many laws which regulate business. Some of those laws can be annoying but must be followed.

Most municipalities have local zoning laws which prohibit business from being conducted in a residential area. Some of the laws do not apply to conducting an online business, as long as people do not come to your home to transact business with you.

There are some organizations like SCORE (Score.org), made up of retired business people, which may be able provide you free information and advice from experienced people who will help you if you plan to set up an actual business to generate income.

Business License.

Some municipalities require you to have a license or permit for certain businesses or to solicit business. Those laws are usually very specific and include many requirements. I found it best to look up that information online rather than asking a local municipal employee. Some employees may incorrectly tell you, that you need a permit or license for anything.

Permits to Sell Food.

Many localities require Health Department permits for selling most food items or for preparing them to resell. Some of those regulations even apply to a child's lemonade stand. Look up those regulations for the municipality where you plan to conduct business.

Sales Tax.

If you are selling anything, most municipalities require you to register for a Tax Identification Number and to collect Local and State Sales Tax. You then must pay that tax to the respective municipality.

Most municipalities require you to file periodic reports showing the amount of sales tax collected accompanied by payment of that amount due. Even if you do not generate any income during a period, you are usually required to file a report, or you will be assessed a penalty.

Income Tax.

All income you receive must be reported when you file your income taxes. In the United States, the Federal Government expects you to file a quarterly report and pay taxes on estimated income.

Too many people conduct business *under the table*. That means they do not report income earned. If you do not report income from items you sell or services you provide you are breaking the law and can be prosecuted.

It is important you keep good records of all income and expenses otherwise you may pay more taxes than what you actually owe.

If you have expenses related to generating income, they reduce the net value of the income you receive. Many of those expenses can be deducted on your taxes so that you pay taxes only on your net gain.

Many people use software to keep track of their income and expenses.

Make sure you set aside some money in case you end up owing additional taxes.

Solicitation.

Many towns require a permit for you to do door-to-door solicitation. Most shopping centers prohibit any solicitation.

Setting Up a Business

If you are going to set up a business there are some essential elements you must consider and address. Some are legal matters. The following advice is not intended to be legal advice but to get you started on the right track.

Get a DBA (Doing Business As).

If you intend to generate income as a business it is usually a good idea to get a DBA (Doing Business As). A DBA is a legal designation which allows you to do business under an assumed name. It can help protect you legally and enables you to open a bank account.

Most DBA's are registered under the primary owner's name and Social Security Number.

A DBA is usually filed with a local authority, such as a county. Some states require you to file with both the county and state.

Always do a search to make sure your desired name is not used in the primary place you will be conducting business. I recommend doing an online search entering the business name you desire to use.

You can use almost any business name which is not registered in your municipality, but which is used in another area. I advise against that. I believe it is best to find a name no one else is using.

After making sure no other business is using the name you desire, I recommend you go to a website domain provider like *GoDaddy* and do a search for the business name you want to use. See if anyone else has that domain. Domain names cannot have spaces or symbols in them.

To search for a domain for *Mike's Marvelous Memorabilia*, you must remember domains containing multiple words do not have spaces between the words. So, you search for *MikesMarvelousMemorabilia*. I recommend using a shorter name like *MarvelousMemorabilia*. If that domain name is not being used, I recommend you buy that domain. They do not cost much through *GoDaddy*.

Set Up a Separate Bank Account.

If you seriously pursue generating additional income, you need to keep good records. To make it simpler it is best to open a separate bank account. You can often do that with the bank you currently do business with. Some banks charge fees for those accounts, some do not.

Set Up a Digital Payment System.

Many people prefer to pay for items digitally using a credit or debit card. It is highly advisable to set up a way to accept digital payments.

Many banks and credit card companies will be glad to set up a merchant account for you. Those accounts often have monthly fees as well as per transaction fees. Those fees can add up.

One good alternative is to use a service like *PayPal*. *PayPal* allows you to receive payments from anyone's debit or credit cards, as well as from other *PayPal* accounts. Currently there are no monthly charges. They only charge a small transaction fee of less than 3%. That is a small cost for generating extra income.

Doing Business

There are certain things you need to understand to conduct business effectively:

Cost and Profit.

You must realize there can be some Costs associated with generating income. That may include supplies, promotion, tools, transportation, or shipping.

Your Profit is the money generated after your expenses.

Though sales tax is based on the total amount of a sale and due and payable in full, income tax is based on the profits you generate

Your expenses are your cost of doing business. Keep track of all your income generating expenses.

You may have the tools, or some supplies necessary to generate income. Keep in mind you may need to replenish supplies or replace tools. Make sure you figure those expenses into your cost of doing business.

You must keep track of your income and expenses, so you can correctly deduct your cost of doing business from your income, otherwise you will pay too much tax.

Shipping.

If you sell things which you need to ship, make sure you charge enough to cover both the packing materials and shipping costs. Check with the *U.S. Postal Service, FedEx* and *UPS* for their rates and requirements.

Many people add the shipping and packing materials to the cost of a transaction as a separate shipping and handling charge. That is not subject to tax.

If you ship items you sell using the *U.S. Postal Service*, they often provide boxes at no cost if you use their *Priority Mail* or *Flat Rate Service*.

You can save money on packing materials if you recycle and repurpose. Save boxes, packing materials and old newspapers.

Supplies.

Find good sources for securing supplies. Lean how to shop for bargains. I address that in my book More than *500 Proven Ways to Reduce Expenses*.

Printing.

You will probably need to print some items. It is helpful

to have some business cards you can give to people.

You may want to print some filers and brochures. When you are first starting you can often do these on your own printer.

Always shop for good values for printing and shipping. I had good success using *VistaPrint* for nice looking low-priced business cards.

You may want to get magnetic signs for your vehicles and maybe some lawn signs. I found significant savings using *VistaPrint* or *StickersBanners.com* for some items verses local print shops.

QR Code.

A QR code is a square digital symbol which directs people who scan it with their phones or tablets to a specific digital address. People do not have type in anything.

You can set up a QR code for free online and put it on your fliers, signs, and business cards.

You should keep an eye out for other useful technological developments.

Selling Products or Services Online

Online selling is changing all the time. It is good to do a search for *selling online* to see what the most effective methods are you can use.

eBay is a great place for selling items. It is a good idea to do some research on the best way to sell on *eBay*.

Craigslist allows you to post items for sale, items wanted, and services offered.

Facebook offers a few ways for you to sell items. You can list them on your own timeline, or you may want to look for Local Flea Market Facebook Sites. Those sites offer the advantage of people picking up items, saving you shipping expenses

Advertising and Publicity

If you want to generate income from some of the methods in this book people need to know what you are selling or what services you provide. You may have great products or provide superior services but if no one knows what you offer, then you will not generate much income.

You Are Your Best Publicity.

It is important how you present yourself. There is a saying, you cannot judge a book by its cover, but many people will judge you by how you look.

Word of Mouth.

Word of mouth is a great way to spread the news. That is where people recommend you to others. Years ago, that was done with in-person encounters. Now that has expanded to include social media or online ratings.

Website.

Years ago, it was necessary to have a geographic place of business where people could find you, and the items you sold, or the services you offered. That has changed. More business is conducted over the internet. For most of the methods in this book you do not need a physical location where people go to conduct business with you.

It is also a good idea to to get a domain name and some kind of website.

I found *GoDaddy* to be the best economic place for me to secure domains and a web presence.

There are some sites which can help you set up a free website. *Wix* is a one of those I used.

With the ever-increasing popularity of social media many people now use a *static website*. That means their website includes an overview of the company, listing of products and services offered, a means to inquire about or purchase those products and services, a means to contact you and a link to social media.

In the past, company news, sales and promotions were included on a website, now many do that on social media.

Make sure you add a payment tab on your website

Social Media.

You need to learn to effectively use social media to maximize your earning potential. This is an area which is constantly changing. Do some online research to discover which social media outlets will work best for you.

Many people supplement their static website with social media. Social media can be used to announce news, sales, and promotions. Many people would rather receive social media updates than have to look for a website.

Two current popular social media platforms you should use are: *Facebook* and *Twitter*.

You may also want to use *LinkedIn* to post an overview of who you are and to keep interested parties informed.

News Releases & News Stories.

Many people still read newspapers, especially the small free local papers. Those are great places to let people know about the products and services you provide.

Newspapers always need news. Learn to write some simple new releases to announce new products or services you offer or successful jobs you accomplished. Include quotations and pictures.

Place some periodic ads in the same papers you send your news releases. Paid advertisers usually get preference for news stories.

Join Associations.

Joining associations related to your field has many benefits. It helps you network with others who have the same interests.

Associations can provide you with sources for new information which can help you be more effective. It can also provide you with credentials.

Over the years I joined many associations including: Historical Associations; Genealogical Associations; Living History Associations; Military Collector Associations; Forensic Associations; and Autograph Associations.

You may want to join an association of local business people. That will help you network and will help keep you abreast of items of local interest which may affect your business. Consider joining such organizations as *Rotary* and your Local Chamber of Commerce.

About the Author

Dr. Larry A. Maxwell is the author of numerous books, including, *More Than 500 Proven Ways to Reduce Expenses*, *More Than 200 Extreme Ways to Reduce Expenses* and *Gaining Personal Financial Freedom*. He has many years of experience and expertise in helping individuals and organizations reduce expenses, save money and generate income.

He is a husband, father, homeowner, pastor, historian, re-enactor, musician, autograph authenticator, consultant, and conference speaker.

He has a wide range of work experience. He started to apply various methods to generate income when he was only 8 years old. He started working a regular job when he was 16 years old when he became one of their youngest managers at Jones Beach as well as the assistant manager of the Jones Beach Theatre where Guy Lombardo conducted the orchestra.

He worked his way through Community College and Graduate School and held various jobs to pay for his schooling and to support his family.

He worked in the accounts payable department for *Caldor*, a billion-dollar retailer, where he negotiated more than $2 million of savings for the company each year.

Be became the top salesperson for *A-Copy America*, which at the time was one of the largest copy machine companies in America.

His writing career started when he became the literary editor for his award winning high school yearbook. He later became a journalist and photographer for *The Times of Ti*, the *Glens Falls Post Star* and the *United Press International*. The *Associated Press* honored his journalism from among all reporters in the United States with its First Place Writing Award.

He travels across America, Canada, Europe, and Asia as a conference speaker. *Gaining Personal Financial Freedom* is one of his popular conferences.

As an outgrowth of his popular Gaining Personal Financial Freedom Seminar, he authored: *112 Proven Ways to Reduce Expenses; Gaining Personal Financial Freedom; Gaining Personal Financial Freedom Budget Workbook;* and the *Gaining Personal Financial Freedom Manual.*

He was a founder and president of *Habitat for Humanity* of Putnam County, New York and President of the *Hudson Valley Trust.*

The Governor of the State of Kentucky honored him for his humanitarian work by conferring on him the title of Kentucky Colonel.

You may contact him to schedule a conference, or for a consultation, or to schedule a speaking engagement at his website LarryMaxwell.com

More Than 150 Proven Ways to Generate Income

Index by Page Number

air	59
alterations	65
animals	155
antique shop	41
antlers	35
art	133, 153
artifacts	27
arrowheads	28
attendant	13
audio books	161
barbwire	30
barnboard	30
beadwork	64
beams	30
bed	180
bell ringer	137
berries	92
bicycles	127
body space	179
bone marrow	179
books	46, 135, 157
book of poetry	155
book of recipes	156
bottles & cans	21, 27
Bounty Hunter	35
Breast milk	176
buckles	29
bullets	28
buttons	29
cannon balls	28
Caregiver	145
cars	114, 127, 131
cattle	102
change in your pocket	19
cheesecake	97
clean homes	117
clean offices	117
clean out basements	42
chickens	97
clinical trials	175
clothing	48, 131
clothing consulting	129
coffee service	82
coins	18
collectables	52, 133
collectables shop	41, 61
companionship	144
commercials	159, 172
cook for others	83
cookies	78
composting	114
consignment	41
contest	92, 141, 152, 155, 173
corn	91
Cosplay	67
costumed service	165
costumes	67, 165
courier service	136
cows	102
Craigslist	34, 38. 40, 61
cremated remains	142
curbside collection	42
cut down trees	111
D.J.	162
deliver flowers	76
detail cars	127
diaper washing	118
different job	15

doll clothing	70	goats	106
doll furniture	71	going out of business	39
doll repairs	70	government job	16
dolls	69	graves	76
door wreaths	78	hair	174
dressings & dips	84	hides	55
dried flowers	77	historical clothing	67
driftwood	27	hogs	101
drive	11, 13	hold signs	109
duck calls	73	home décor	49, 133
dumps	38	horns	58
eBay	40, 61	host the flu	180
elected office	17	instrument	167
coins	18	items of local interest	46
cupcakes	80	jam or jelly	93
eggs	97	jewelry	26
family history	155	laundry service	117
find people	34	lease body space	179
firewood	111	*Lift*	11
fish	85	Live-in Companion	145
Fiverr	108	*Living History Guild*	68
flea markets	39, 61	Local events	171
fliers	108	lost items	34
flowers	75	luggage carts	108
flower arrangements	77	lunch deliveries	82
flu	180	make overs	128
food cart	82	maple syrup	93
fossils	26	memorabilia	40
free things	36	memorial displays	74
Freecycle	37	memory displays	75
fruit trees	96	metal detector	25, 28
fudge	81	meteorites	24
funerals	14, 171	milk	102
furniture	133	model	162
garden	87	*Moirologist*	14
genealogy	125, 155	Mourner	14
generators	113	movie extra	160
gifts	132	mow lawns	110

More Than 150 Proven Ways to Generate Income

music	167, 172
musket balls	28
nails	29
NASA	180
necessities	131
needlework	62
News Correspondent	158
newspapers	109, 120
nut trees	96
pawn shops	41
Pallbearer	13
pan for gold	23
parties	171
pass out fliers	108
patch holes & tears	65
Personal Shopper	130
pet parties	140
Pet Sitter	139
Pet Walker	138
pets	138
phone calls	110
photo book of people	154
photo book of animals	155
photo conversion	125
photo history book	152
photos	120, 152
pianos	53
pictures	119
pies	97
pigs	101
plasma	174
play an instrument	167
poetry	155
postcards	43
power wash	115
Product Tester	172
Process Server	12
publish artwork	153
publish family history	155
publish photographs	152
publish poetry	155
publish recipes	156
puppets	69
QR code	170
Quilts	63
rabbits	100
railroad spikes	32
recipes	156
recycling center	38
relics	27
remove larger items	116
republish old books	157
replace buttons	65
repossess	12
research studies	173
restaurants	171
roadkill	14, 56
Roadkill Collector	14
rocks & minerals	23, 59
Salvation Army bell	137
sand	59
scrimshaw	73
seashells	26
seeds	91
second job	12
selected buyers	42
sell things for others	60
sell your bone marrow	179
sell your hair	174
sell your plasma	174
sewing	66
sewing repairs	65
sheep	104
shopping carts	108
shovel cars	114
Shovler	114

shredding	136	turtles	84
signs	109, 175	*Uber*	11
sing	167	update old books	157
SnoHub	114	vacation transport	137
stamps	52	vegetables	86
stay in bed	180	vintage clothing	48
sweepstakes	173	wash windows	115
tag sale	37, 39, 41, 61	water	59
take pictures	119	weaving	63
talent show	163	weddings	171
TaskRabbit	111	windows	31
technology	131	wooden items	71
telephone insulators	33	work different shift	10
temporary agency	11	work additional day	10
thrift shops	39	work additional hours	9
toy restoration	72	work for food sign	175
trading cards	50	work for yourself	9
transfer	10	write & publish	145
trash cans	116	write fiction	150
travel	134	write music	172
trees	111	write non-fiction	151
tune bicycles	127	yard work	111

www.ingramcontent.com/pod-product-compliance
Lightning Source LLC
Chambersburg PA
CBHW071913110526
44591CB00011B/1667